50 Classic American Dessert Recipes for Home

By: Kelly Johnson

Table of Contents

- Apple Pie
- Chocolate Chip Cookies
- New York Cheesecake
- Key Lime Pie
- Red Velvet Cake
- Pecan Pie
- Banana Bread
- Blueberry Cobbler
- Carrot Cake
- Chocolate Brownies
- Lemon Bars
- Peanut Butter Cookies
- Strawberry Shortcake
- Boston Cream Pie
- Pineapple Upside-Down Cake
- Mississippi Mud Pie
- Black Forest Cake
- Coconut Cream Pie
- S'mores Bars
- Oatmeal Raisin Cookies
- Peach Cobbler
- Pumpkin Pie
- Snickerdoodles
- Tiramisu
- Cherry Pie
- Chocolate Mousse
- Whoopie Pies
- Cinnamon Rolls
- Bread Pudding
- Angel Food Cake
- Ice Cream Sandwiches
- Apple Crisp
- Raspberry Cheesecake Bars
- Blondies
- Lemon Meringue Pie

- Fudge Brownies
- Texas Sheet Cake
- Strawberry Rhubarb Pie
- Buttermilk Pie
- Coconut Macaroons
- Gooey Butter Cake
- M&M Cookies
- Peanut Butter Pie
- Chocolate Eclairs
- Blackberry Cobbler
- Apple Dumplings
- Chocolate Covered Strawberries
- Rice Krispie Treats
- Molten Lava Cake
- Lemon Pound Cake

Apple Pie

Ingredients:

For the crust:

- 2 ½ cups all-purpose flour
- 1 cup (2 sticks) cold unsalted butter, cubed
- 1 teaspoon salt
- 1 tablespoon granulated sugar
- 6-8 tablespoons ice water

For the filling:

- 6-7 large apples (such as Granny Smith or Honeycrisp), peeled, cored, and thinly sliced
- ¾ cup granulated sugar
- 2 tablespoons all-purpose flour
- 1 teaspoon ground cinnamon
- ¼ teaspoon ground nutmeg
- 1 tablespoon lemon juice
- 2 tablespoons unsalted butter, cut into small pieces
- 1 egg, beaten (for egg wash)
- 1 tablespoon granulated sugar (for sprinkling)

Instructions:

1. Prepare the Crust:
    - In a large mixing bowl, combine the flour, salt, and sugar. Add the cold cubed butter.
    - Use a pastry cutter or your fingers to work the butter into the flour mixture until it resembles coarse crumbs.
    - Gradually add the ice water, 1 tablespoon at a time, mixing with a fork until the dough just begins to come together.
    - Divide the dough in half and shape each half into a disk. Wrap each disk tightly in plastic wrap and refrigerate for at least 1 hour, or overnight.
2. Prepare the Filling:
    - In a large bowl, toss the sliced apples with lemon juice to prevent browning.

- In a separate bowl, mix together the granulated sugar, flour, cinnamon, and nutmeg. Add this mixture to the apples and toss until the apples are evenly coated.
3. Assemble the Pie:
    - Preheat your oven to 375°F (190°C). Place a baking sheet on the lower rack to catch any drips.
    - On a lightly floured surface, roll out one disk of dough into a circle large enough to line a 9-inch pie dish. Carefully transfer the dough to the pie dish and press it gently into the bottom and sides.
    - Pour the apple filling into the pie crust, mounding it slightly in the center. Dot the top with pieces of butter.
    - Roll out the second disk of dough and place it over the filling. Trim any excess dough and crimp the edges to seal. Cut slits in the top crust to allow steam to escape.
    - Brush the top crust with beaten egg and sprinkle with granulated sugar.
4. Bake the Pie:
    - Place the pie on the preheated baking sheet in the oven and bake for 45-55 minutes, or until the crust is golden brown and the filling is bubbly.
    - If the edges of the crust begin to brown too quickly, cover them with aluminum foil or a pie shield.
    - Once baked, remove the pie from the oven and allow it to cool on a wire rack for at least 1 hour before serving.
5. Serve:
    - Serve the apple pie warm or at room temperature, optionally with a scoop of vanilla ice cream or a dollop of whipped cream. Enjoy!

Chocolate Chip Cookies

Ingredients:

- 1 cup (2 sticks) unsalted butter, softened
- 3/4 cup granulated sugar
- 3/4 cup packed light brown sugar
- 2 large eggs
- 1 teaspoon vanilla extract
- 2 1/4 cups all-purpose flour
- 1 teaspoon baking soda
- 1/2 teaspoon salt
- 2 cups semisweet chocolate chips

Instructions:

1. Preheat Oven and Prepare Baking Sheets:
    - Preheat your oven to 375°F (190°C). Line baking sheets with parchment paper or silicone baking mats.
2. Cream Butter and Sugars:
    - In a large mixing bowl, cream together the softened butter, granulated sugar, and brown sugar until light and fluffy, about 2-3 minutes with a hand mixer or stand mixer.
3. Add Eggs and Vanilla:
    - Add the eggs one at a time, mixing well after each addition. Mix in the vanilla extract until well combined.
4. Combine Dry Ingredients:
    - In a separate bowl, whisk together the all-purpose flour, baking soda, and salt.
5. Combine Wet and Dry Ingredients:
    - Gradually add the dry ingredients to the wet ingredients, mixing until just combined. Be careful not to overmix.
6. Add Chocolate Chips:
    - Stir in the semisweet chocolate chips until evenly distributed throughout the cookie dough.
7. Scoop Dough onto Baking Sheets:
    - Drop rounded tablespoons of cookie dough onto the prepared baking sheets, spacing them about 2 inches apart to allow for spreading.
8. Bake:

- Bake the cookies in the preheated oven for 8-10 minutes, or until the edges are lightly golden brown. The centers may still look slightly soft, but they will continue to set as they cool.
9. Cool and Serve:
    - Allow the cookies to cool on the baking sheets for a few minutes before transferring them to a wire rack to cool completely. Enjoy your delicious homemade chocolate chip cookies!
10. Storage:
- Store any leftover cookies in an airtight container at room temperature for up to 5 days. You can also freeze the baked cookies for longer storage, placing them in a freezer-safe container or bag for up to 2-3 months.

New York Cheesecake

Ingredients:

For the crust:

- 1 1/2 cups graham cracker crumbs
- 1/4 cup granulated sugar
- 1/2 cup (1 stick) unsalted butter, melted

For the filling:

- 32 oz (4 packages) cream cheese, at room temperature
- 1 1/4 cups granulated sugar
- 4 large eggs, at room temperature
- 1 cup sour cream, at room temperature
- 1 tablespoon vanilla extract
- 1/4 cup all-purpose flour
- Zest of 1 lemon (optional)

Instructions:

1. Preheat Oven and Prepare Pan:
    - Preheat your oven to 325°F (160°C). Wrap the outside of a 9-inch springform pan with aluminum foil to prevent any leaks.
2. Make the Crust:
    - In a medium bowl, mix together the graham cracker crumbs, sugar, and melted butter until well combined. Press the mixture evenly into the bottom of the prepared springform pan.
3. Prepare the Filling:
    - In a large mixing bowl, beat the cream cheese and sugar together until smooth and creamy, about 3-4 minutes, scraping down the sides of the bowl as needed.
    - Add the eggs one at a time, beating well after each addition. Mix in the sour cream, vanilla extract, and flour until smooth. Fold in the lemon zest, if using.
4. Bake the Cheesecake:

- Pour the filling over the prepared crust in the springform pan. Tap the pan gently on the counter to release any air bubbles.
- Place the springform pan in a larger baking pan and fill the larger pan with hot water until it reaches about halfway up the sides of the springform pan. This water bath will help prevent cracking.
- Bake the cheesecake in the preheated oven for 55-65 minutes, or until the edges are set but the center still jiggles slightly.
- Turn off the oven and leave the cheesecake inside with the door closed for 1 hour to cool gradually. This helps prevent cracking as well.

5. Chill and Serve:
    - Remove the cheesecake from the oven and let it cool completely on a wire rack. Once cooled, cover the cheesecake with plastic wrap and refrigerate for at least 4 hours or overnight until well chilled and set.
    - Before serving, run a knife around the edges of the cheesecake to loosen it from the pan. Carefully remove the sides of the springform pan.
    - Slice the cheesecake into wedges and serve chilled. Enjoy the rich and creamy goodness of New York Cheesecake!

Key Lime Pie

Ingredients:

For the crust:

- 1 1/2 cups graham cracker crumbs
- 1/4 cup granulated sugar
- 1/2 cup (1 stick) unsalted butter, melted

For the filling:

- 4 large egg yolks
- 1 can (14 ounces) sweetened condensed milk
- 1/2 cup freshly squeezed key lime juice (about 20-25 key limes)
- Zest of 1-2 key limes (optional)

For the topping (optional):

- 1 cup heavy whipping cream
- 2 tablespoons powdered sugar
- Lime slices or zest for garnish

Instructions:

1. Preheat Oven and Prepare Pan:
    - Preheat your oven to 350°F (175°C). Grease a 9-inch pie dish with butter or non-stick cooking spray.
2. Make the Crust:
    - In a mixing bowl, combine the graham cracker crumbs, granulated sugar, and melted butter. Mix until well combined and the mixture resembles wet sand.
    - Press the mixture firmly and evenly into the bottom and up the sides of the prepared pie dish.
3. Bake the Crust:

- Bake the crust in the preheated oven for 10-12 minutes, or until lightly golden brown. Remove from the oven and let it cool while you prepare the filling.
4. Make the Filling:
    - In a large mixing bowl, whisk together the egg yolks and sweetened condensed milk until smooth.
    - Gradually add the key lime juice, whisking continuously, until well combined. Stir in the key lime zest, if using.
5. Pour Filling into Crust:
    - Pour the filling into the cooled graham cracker crust, spreading it evenly with a spatula.
6. Bake the Pie:
    - Return the pie to the oven and bake for 10-12 minutes, or until the filling is just set. It should still have a slight jiggle in the center.
7. Cool and Chill:
    - Remove the pie from the oven and let it cool to room temperature on a wire rack. Once cooled, cover the pie with plastic wrap and refrigerate for at least 4 hours or overnight until well chilled and set.
8. Optional Topping:
    - In a mixing bowl, whip the heavy whipping cream and powdered sugar until stiff peaks form. Spread the whipped cream over the chilled pie.
    - Garnish with lime slices or zest, if desired.
9. Serve:
    - Slice the Key Lime Pie and serve chilled. Enjoy the tangy and refreshing flavor of this classic dessert!

Red Velvet Cake

Ingredients:

For the cake:

- 2 1/2 cups all-purpose flour
- 1 1/2 cups granulated sugar
- 1 teaspoon baking soda
- 1 teaspoon salt
- 2 tablespoons unsweetened cocoa powder
- 1 cup vegetable oil
- 1 cup buttermilk, at room temperature
- 2 large eggs, at room temperature
- 2 tablespoons red food coloring
- 1 teaspoon white vinegar
- 1 teaspoon vanilla extract

For the cream cheese frosting:

- 16 ounces cream cheese, softened
- 1/2 cup (1 stick) unsalted butter, softened
- 4 cups powdered sugar, sifted
- 1 teaspoon vanilla extract

Instructions:

1. Preheat Oven and Prepare Cake Pans:
    - Preheat your oven to 350°F (175°C). Grease and flour two 9-inch round cake pans or line them with parchment paper.
2. Make the Cake Batter:
    - In a large mixing bowl, sift together the flour, sugar, baking soda, salt, and cocoa powder.
    - In another bowl, whisk together the vegetable oil, buttermilk, eggs, red food coloring, vinegar, and vanilla extract until well combined.
    - Gradually add the wet ingredients to the dry ingredients, mixing until just combined and no lumps remain.

3. Bake the Cake:
   - Divide the cake batter evenly between the prepared cake pans.
   - Bake in the preheated oven for 25-30 minutes, or until a toothpick inserted into the center of the cakes comes out clean.
   - Remove the cakes from the oven and let them cool in the pans for 10 minutes before transferring them to wire racks to cool completely.
4. Make the Cream Cheese Frosting:
   - In a large mixing bowl, beat the softened cream cheese and butter together until smooth and creamy.
   - Gradually add the powdered sugar, mixing on low speed until well combined and smooth.
   - Mix in the vanilla extract until incorporated.
5. Assemble the Cake:
   - Once the cakes have cooled completely, place one cake layer on a serving plate or cake stand.
   - Spread a layer of cream cheese frosting evenly over the top of the first cake layer.
   - Place the second cake layer on top and frost the top and sides of the cake with the remaining cream cheese frosting.
6. Decorate (Optional):
   - If desired, crumble one of the cake layers and sprinkle the crumbs over the top of the frosted cake for decoration.
   - You can also garnish with fresh berries or chocolate shavings if desired.
7. Chill and Serve:
   - Chill the cake in the refrigerator for at least 30 minutes before slicing and serving to allow the frosting to set.
   - Serve slices of delicious Red Velvet Cake and enjoy the rich, moist texture and tangy cream cheese frosting!

Pecan Pie

Ingredients:

For the crust:

- 1 1/4 cups all-purpose flour
- 1/2 teaspoon salt
- 1/2 teaspoon granulated sugar
- 1/2 cup (1 stick) cold unsalted butter, cut into small pieces
- 2-4 tablespoons ice water

For the filling:

- 1 cup granulated sugar
- 1 cup light corn syrup
- 1/2 teaspoon salt
- 3 large eggs
- 1 teaspoon vanilla extract
- 2 tablespoons unsalted butter, melted
- 1 1/2 cups pecan halves

Instructions:

1. Make the Crust:
    - In a large mixing bowl, combine the flour, salt, and sugar. Add the cold butter pieces and use a pastry cutter or your fingers to work the butter into the flour mixture until it resembles coarse crumbs.
    - Gradually add the ice water, 1 tablespoon at a time, mixing until the dough just comes together and forms a ball.
    - Shape the dough into a disk, wrap it tightly in plastic wrap, and refrigerate for at least 30 minutes.
2. Preheat Oven:
    - Preheat your oven to 375°F (190°C).
3. Roll Out the Crust:
    - On a lightly floured surface, roll out the chilled dough into a circle about 12 inches in diameter. Carefully transfer the dough to a 9-inch pie dish and press it gently into the bottom and up the sides. Trim any excess dough and crimp the edges as desired.

4. Prepare the Filling:
   - In a medium mixing bowl, whisk together the granulated sugar, corn syrup, salt, eggs, vanilla extract, and melted butter until well combined.
   - Stir in the pecan halves until they are evenly coated in the filling mixture.
5. Assemble and Bake:
   - Pour the pecan filling into the prepared pie crust, spreading it out evenly.
   - Place the pie on a baking sheet to catch any potential spills and bake in the preheated oven for 45-50 minutes, or until the filling is set and the crust is golden brown.
   - If the edges of the crust start to brown too quickly, you can cover them with aluminum foil or a pie shield halfway through baking.
6. Cool and Serve:
   - Remove the pie from the oven and let it cool completely on a wire rack before slicing and serving.
   - Serve slices of delicious Pecan Pie with a dollop of whipped cream or a scoop of vanilla ice cream, if desired. Enjoy the rich, nutty flavor and gooey texture of this classic Southern dessert!

Banana Bread

Ingredients:

- 2-3 ripe bananas, mashed (about 1 cup)
- 1/2 cup (1 stick) unsalted butter, melted
- 3/4 cup granulated sugar
- 2 large eggs
- 1 teaspoon vanilla extract
- 1 1/2 cups all-purpose flour
- 1 teaspoon baking soda
- 1/2 teaspoon salt
- 1/2 teaspoon ground cinnamon (optional)
- 1/2 cup chopped nuts (such as walnuts or pecans), chocolate chips, or dried fruit (optional)

Instructions:

1. Preheat Oven:
   - Preheat your oven to 350°F (175°C). Grease a 9x5-inch loaf pan or line it with parchment paper.
2. Prepare Wet Ingredients:
   - In a large mixing bowl, mash the ripe bananas with a fork or potato masher until smooth.
   - Add the melted butter and granulated sugar to the mashed bananas, and mix until well combined.
3. Add Eggs and Vanilla:
   - Beat in the eggs, one at a time, until incorporated.
   - Stir in the vanilla extract until smooth.
4. Combine Dry Ingredients:
   - In a separate bowl, whisk together the all-purpose flour, baking soda, salt, and ground cinnamon (if using).
5. Combine Wet and Dry Ingredients:
   - Gradually add the dry ingredients to the wet ingredients, stirring until just combined. Be careful not to overmix.
   - If using, fold in the chopped nuts, chocolate chips, or dried fruit until evenly distributed throughout the batter.
6. Bake:

- Pour the batter into the prepared loaf pan and smooth the top with a spatula.
- Bake in the preheated oven for 55-65 minutes, or until a toothpick inserted into the center comes out clean.
- If the top starts to brown too quickly, you can tent the loaf pan with aluminum foil halfway through baking.

7. Cool and Serve:
    - Once baked, remove the banana bread from the oven and let it cool in the pan for 10-15 minutes.
    - Carefully transfer the banana bread to a wire rack to cool completely before slicing.
    - Slice and serve the banana bread warm or at room temperature. Enjoy the moist and flavorful treat!

Blueberry Cobbler

Ingredients:

For the filling:

- 4 cups fresh or frozen blueberries
- 1/2 cup granulated sugar
- 1 tablespoon lemon juice
- 1 teaspoon lemon zest (optional)
- 1 tablespoon cornstarch

For the topping:

- 1 cup all-purpose flour
- 1/4 cup granulated sugar
- 1 teaspoon baking powder
- 1/4 teaspoon salt
- 1/2 cup (1 stick) unsalted butter, cold and cut into small pieces
- 1/4 cup boiling water

Instructions:

1. Preheat Oven:
    - Preheat your oven to 375°F (190°C). Lightly grease a 9x9-inch baking dish or similar-sized casserole dish.
2. Prepare the Filling:
    - In a large mixing bowl, combine the blueberries, granulated sugar, lemon juice, lemon zest (if using), and cornstarch. Toss until the blueberries are evenly coated. Pour the mixture into the prepared baking dish and spread it out evenly.
3. Make the Topping:
    - In a separate mixing bowl, whisk together the flour, granulated sugar, baking powder, and salt.
    - Cut in the cold butter using a pastry cutter, fork, or your fingers until the mixture resembles coarse crumbs.
    - Pour the boiling water over the flour mixture and stir until just combined. The dough will be thick and sticky.
4. Add Topping to Filling:

- Drop spoonfuls of the topping over the blueberry filling, covering it as evenly as possible. The topping will spread as it bakes.
5. Bake:
    - Place the baking dish in the preheated oven and bake for 35-40 minutes, or until the topping is golden brown and the filling is bubbling around the edges.
6. Cool and Serve:
    - Remove the blueberry cobbler from the oven and let it cool for a few minutes before serving.
    - Serve warm, either plain or with a scoop of vanilla ice cream or a dollop of whipped cream if desired. Enjoy the sweet and tangy flavors of this delicious dessert!

Carrot Cake

Ingredients:

For the cake:

- 2 cups all-purpose flour
- 2 teaspoons baking powder
- 1 teaspoon baking soda
- 1/2 teaspoon salt
- 2 teaspoons ground cinnamon
- 1/2 teaspoon ground nutmeg
- 1 cup granulated sugar
- 1 cup brown sugar, packed
- 1 cup vegetable oil
- 4 large eggs
- 2 teaspoons vanilla extract
- 2 cups grated carrots (about 3-4 medium carrots)
- 1 cup crushed pineapple, drained
- 1 cup chopped walnuts or pecans (optional)
- 1/2 cup shredded coconut (optional)

For the cream cheese frosting:

- 1/2 cup (1 stick) unsalted butter, softened
- 8 ounces cream cheese, softened
- 4 cups powdered sugar
- 1 teaspoon vanilla extract

Instructions:

1. Preheat Oven and Prepare Pans:
    - Preheat your oven to 350°F (175°C). Grease and flour two 9-inch round cake pans or line them with parchment paper.
2. Mix Dry Ingredients:
    - In a large mixing bowl, sift together the flour, baking powder, baking soda, salt, cinnamon, and nutmeg. Set aside.
3. Mix Wet Ingredients:

- In another bowl, whisk together the granulated sugar, brown sugar, vegetable oil, eggs, and vanilla extract until well combined.
4. Combine Wet and Dry Ingredients:
    - Gradually add the wet ingredients to the dry ingredients, mixing until just combined.
    - Fold in the grated carrots, crushed pineapple, chopped nuts (if using), and shredded coconut (if using) until evenly distributed throughout the batter.
5. Bake the Cake:
    - Divide the batter evenly between the prepared cake pans.
    - Bake in the preheated oven for 25-30 minutes, or until a toothpick inserted into the center of the cakes comes out clean.
    - Remove the cakes from the oven and let them cool in the pans for 10 minutes before transferring them to wire racks to cool completely.
6. Make the Cream Cheese Frosting:
    - In a large mixing bowl, beat the softened butter and cream cheese together until smooth and creamy.
    - Gradually add the powdered sugar, mixing on low speed until well combined and smooth.
    - Stir in the vanilla extract until incorporated.
7. Assemble the Cake:
    - Once the cakes have cooled completely, place one cake layer on a serving plate or cake stand.
    - Spread a layer of cream cheese frosting evenly over the top of the first cake layer.
    - Place the second cake layer on top and frost the top and sides of the cake with the remaining cream cheese frosting.
8. Decorate (Optional):
    - You can decorate the top of the cake with additional shredded coconut or chopped nuts if desired.
9. Chill and Serve:
    - Chill the cake in the refrigerator for at least 30 minutes before slicing and serving to allow the frosting to set.
    - Serve slices of delicious Carrot Cake and enjoy the moist and flavorful treat!

Chocolate Brownies

Ingredients:

- 1 cup (2 sticks) unsalted butter
- 2 cups granulated sugar
- 4 large eggs
- 2 teaspoons vanilla extract
- 1 cup all-purpose flour
- 3/4 cup unsweetened cocoa powder
- 1/2 teaspoon salt
- 1 cup semisweet chocolate chips (optional)
- 1/2 cup chopped nuts, such as walnuts or pecans (optional)

Instructions:

1. Preheat Oven and Prepare Pan:
    - Preheat your oven to 350°F (175°C). Grease a 9x13-inch baking pan or line it with parchment paper.
2. Melt Butter:
    - In a medium saucepan, melt the butter over low heat. Remove from heat once melted.
3. Mix Wet Ingredients:
    - In a large mixing bowl, combine the melted butter and granulated sugar. Stir until well combined.
    - Add the eggs one at a time, mixing well after each addition.
    - Stir in the vanilla extract until smooth.
4. Add Dry Ingredients:
    - Sift the flour, cocoa powder, and salt into the wet ingredients. Stir until just combined. Be careful not to overmix.
    - If using, fold in the chocolate chips and chopped nuts until evenly distributed throughout the batter.
5. Bake:
    - Pour the batter into the prepared baking pan and spread it out evenly with a spatula.
    - Bake in the preheated oven for 25-30 minutes, or until a toothpick inserted into the center comes out with a few moist crumbs. Be careful not to overbake, as brownies should be moist and fudgy.

6. Cool and Serve:
    - Remove the brownies from the oven and let them cool completely in the pan on a wire rack.
    - Once cooled, cut the brownies into squares or rectangles and serve. Enjoy the rich and chocolaty goodness of homemade brownies!

These brownies are perfect for any occasion and can be enjoyed on their own or with a scoop of ice cream for an extra treat.

Lemon Bars

Ingredients:

For the crust:

- 1 cup all-purpose flour
- 1/4 cup granulated sugar
- 1/2 cup (1 stick) unsalted butter, cold and cut into small pieces

For the lemon filling:

- 4 large eggs
- 1 1/2 cups granulated sugar
- 1/2 cup freshly squeezed lemon juice (about 3-4 lemons)
- Zest of 2 lemons
- 1/4 cup all-purpose flour
- Powdered sugar, for dusting

Instructions:

1. Preheat Oven and Prepare Pan:
    - Preheat your oven to 350°F (175°C). Grease or line a 9x13-inch baking pan with parchment paper, leaving an overhang for easy removal.
2. Make the Crust:
    - In a mixing bowl, combine the flour and granulated sugar. Cut in the cold butter using a pastry cutter or your fingers until the mixture resembles coarse crumbs.
    - Press the crust mixture evenly into the bottom of the prepared baking pan.
3. Bake the Crust:
    - Bake the crust in the preheated oven for 15-18 minutes, or until lightly golden brown around the edges. Remove from the oven and set aside.
4. Make the Lemon Filling:
    - In a separate mixing bowl, whisk together the eggs, granulated sugar, lemon juice, lemon zest, and flour until well combined and smooth.
5. Pour Filling Over Crust:

- Pour the lemon filling over the baked crust, spreading it out evenly with a spatula.
6. Bake Again:
    - Return the pan to the oven and bake for an additional 20-25 minutes, or until the filling is set and the edges are lightly golden brown.
7. Cool and Chill:
    - Remove the pan from the oven and let the lemon bars cool completely in the pan on a wire rack.
    - Once cooled, refrigerate the lemon bars for at least 2 hours, or until well chilled and set.
8. Slice and Serve:
    - Use the parchment paper overhang to lift the chilled lemon bars out of the pan. Dust the top with powdered sugar.
    - Cut the lemon bars into squares or rectangles using a sharp knife. Serve chilled and enjoy the tangy and refreshing flavor of these homemade lemon bars!

Peanut Butter Cookies

Ingredients:

- 1 cup creamy peanut butter
- 1/2 cup granulated sugar
- 1/2 cup packed light brown sugar
- 1 large egg
- 1 teaspoon vanilla extract
- 1/2 teaspoon baking soda
- 1/4 teaspoon salt

Instructions:

1. Preheat Oven:
    - Preheat your oven to 350°F (175°C). Line a baking sheet with parchment paper or silicone baking mat.
2. Mix Wet Ingredients:
    - In a large mixing bowl, beat together the creamy peanut butter, granulated sugar, and brown sugar until well combined and creamy.
3. Add Egg and Vanilla:
    - Beat in the egg and vanilla extract until smooth.
4. Add Dry Ingredients:
    - Add the baking soda and salt to the peanut butter mixture, and mix until well combined.
5. Form Cookie Dough Balls:
    - Roll the dough into tablespoon-sized balls and place them onto the prepared baking sheet. You can use a fork to create a crisscross pattern on the top of each cookie if desired, flattening them slightly.
6. Bake:
    - Bake the cookies in the preheated oven for 8-10 minutes, or until the edges are golden brown. The centers may still look slightly soft, but they will continue to set as they cool.
7. Cool and Serve:
    - Allow the cookies to cool on the baking sheet for a few minutes before transferring them to a wire rack to cool completely.
    - Once cooled, serve and enjoy these deliciously chewy Peanut Butter Cookies!

These cookies are perfect for peanut butter lovers and make a delightful treat for any occasion. You can also add chocolate chips or chopped nuts to the dough for extra flavor and texture if desired.

Strawberry Shortcake

Ingredients:

For the shortcakes:

- 2 cups all-purpose flour
- 1/4 cup granulated sugar
- 1 tablespoon baking powder
- 1/2 teaspoon salt
- 1/2 cup (1 stick) cold unsalted butter, cut into small pieces
- 3/4 cup cold heavy cream
- 1 teaspoon vanilla extract

For the strawberries:

- 1 1/2 pounds fresh strawberries, hulled and sliced
- 2-4 tablespoons granulated sugar (adjust to taste)
- 1 teaspoon lemon juice (optional)

For the whipped cream:

- 1 cup cold heavy cream
- 2 tablespoons powdered sugar
- 1 teaspoon vanilla extract

Instructions:

1. Preheat Oven:
    - Preheat your oven to 400°F (200°C). Line a baking sheet with parchment paper.
2. Make the Shortcakes:
    - In a large mixing bowl, whisk together the flour, sugar, baking powder, and salt.
    - Cut in the cold butter using a pastry cutter or your fingers until the mixture resembles coarse crumbs.
    - In a small bowl, mix together the cold heavy cream and vanilla extract.

- Gradually add the cream mixture to the flour mixture, stirring until the dough comes together.
- Turn the dough out onto a lightly floured surface and gently knead it a few times until it holds together.
- Pat the dough into a circle about 1 inch thick. Use a round cookie cutter or glass to cut out shortcakes. Place them onto the prepared baking sheet.

3. Bake the Shortcakes:
   - Bake in the preheated oven for 12-15 minutes, or until the shortcakes are golden brown. Remove from the oven and let them cool on a wire rack.
4. Prepare the Strawberries:
   - In a mixing bowl, toss the sliced strawberries with granulated sugar and lemon juice (if using). Let them macerate for about 15-20 minutes to release their juices.
5. Make the Whipped Cream:
   - In a chilled mixing bowl, beat the cold heavy cream, powdered sugar, and vanilla extract until stiff peaks form.
6. Assemble the Strawberry Shortcakes:
   - Slice the cooled shortcakes in half horizontally.
   - Spoon some of the macerated strawberries onto the bottom half of each shortcake.
   - Top with a dollop of whipped cream.
   - Place the top halves of the shortcakes over the whipped cream.
   - Garnish with additional strawberries and a dusting of powdered sugar if desired.
7. Serve:
   - Serve the Strawberry Shortcakes immediately and enjoy the delicious combination of sweet strawberries, fluffy shortcakes, and whipped cream!

Boston Cream Pie

Ingredients:

For the cake:

- 1 cup all-purpose flour
- 1 teaspoon baking powder
- 1/4 teaspoon salt
- 4 large eggs, at room temperature
- 1 cup granulated sugar
- 1/2 cup whole milk
- 1 teaspoon vanilla extract

For the pastry cream filling:

- 2 cups whole milk
- 1/2 cup granulated sugar
- 4 large egg yolks
- 1/4 cup cornstarch
- 1/4 teaspoon salt
- 2 teaspoons vanilla extract

For the chocolate ganache topping:

- 4 ounces semisweet chocolate, chopped
- 1/2 cup heavy cream

Instructions:

1. Preheat Oven and Prepare Pan:
   - Preheat your oven to 350°F (175°C). Grease and flour two 9-inch round cake pans or line them with parchment paper.
2. Make the Cake:
   - In a mixing bowl, sift together the flour, baking powder, and salt. Set aside.
   - In another mixing bowl, beat the eggs and granulated sugar together until pale and fluffy, about 3-4 minutes.

- Stir in the milk and vanilla extract until well combined.
- Gradually add the dry ingredients to the wet ingredients, mixing until just combined.
- Divide the batter evenly between the prepared cake pans.
- Bake in the preheated oven for 20-25 minutes, or until a toothpick inserted into the center of the cakes comes out clean.
- Remove the cakes from the oven and let them cool in the pans for 10 minutes before transferring them to wire racks to cool completely.

3. Make the Pastry Cream Filling:
    - In a saucepan, heat the milk over medium heat until steaming but not boiling.
    - In a mixing bowl, whisk together the granulated sugar, egg yolks, cornstarch, and salt until smooth and pale.
    - Gradually whisk the hot milk into the egg mixture.
    - Return the mixture to the saucepan and cook over medium heat, whisking constantly, until thickened.
    - Remove from heat and stir in the vanilla extract.
    - Transfer the pastry cream to a bowl and cover it with plastic wrap, pressing the plastic wrap directly onto the surface to prevent a skin from forming. Chill in the refrigerator until cold.

4. Assemble the Cake:
    - Once the cakes and pastry cream are cooled, place one cake layer on a serving plate or cake stand.
    - Spread the chilled pastry cream evenly over the top of the cake layer.
    - Place the second cake layer on top.

5. Make the Chocolate Ganache Topping:
    - Place the chopped semisweet chocolate in a heatproof bowl.
    - In a saucepan, heat the heavy cream over medium heat until it just begins to simmer.
    - Pour the hot cream over the chopped chocolate and let it sit for 1-2 minutes.
    - Stir the chocolate and cream together until smooth and glossy.

6. Top the Cake:
    - Pour the chocolate ganache over the top of the assembled cake, allowing it to drip down the sides.
    - Let the ganache set for a few minutes before slicing and serving.

7. Serve:

- Slice the Boston Cream Pie and serve it chilled or at room temperature. Enjoy the decadent layers of sponge cake, creamy pastry cream, and rich chocolate ganache!

Pineapple Upside-Down Cake

Ingredients:

For the topping:

- 1/4 cup (1/2 stick) unsalted butter
- 3/4 cup packed brown sugar
- 7-8 canned pineapple rings, drained
- Maraschino cherries, drained (optional)

For the cake:

- 1 1/2 cups all-purpose flour
- 1 teaspoon baking powder
- 1/4 teaspoon salt
- 1/2 cup (1 stick) unsalted butter, softened
- 1 cup granulated sugar
- 2 large eggs
- 1 teaspoon vanilla extract
- 1/2 cup pineapple juice (reserved from the canned pineapple)
- 1/4 cup whole milk or buttermilk

Instructions:

1. Preheat Oven and Prepare Pan:
    - Preheat your oven to 350°F (175°C). Grease a 9-inch round cake pan.
2. Make the Topping:
    - In a small saucepan, melt the butter over medium heat.
    - Add the brown sugar and stir until dissolved and bubbly.
    - Pour the mixture into the prepared cake pan and spread it out evenly.
    - Arrange the pineapple rings on top of the brown sugar mixture, placing a maraschino cherry in the center of each ring (if using).
3. Make the Cake Batter:
    - In a mixing bowl, sift together the flour, baking powder, and salt. Set aside.
    - In another mixing bowl, cream together the softened butter and granulated sugar until light and fluffy.

- Beat in the eggs, one at a time, until well combined. Stir in the vanilla extract.
- Gradually add the dry ingredients to the wet ingredients, alternating with the pineapple juice and milk, beginning and ending with the dry ingredients. Mix until just combined.

4. Assemble and Bake:
   - Carefully pour the cake batter over the pineapple rings and brown sugar mixture in the cake pan, spreading it out evenly.
5. Bake the Cake:
   - Bake in the preheated oven for 40-45 minutes, or until a toothpick inserted into the center of the cake comes out clean.
6. Cool and Invert:
   - Remove the cake from the oven and let it cool in the pan for 5-10 minutes.
   - Place a serving plate over the top of the cake pan and carefully invert the cake onto the plate. Tap the bottom of the pan to release the cake, then carefully lift off the pan.
7. Serve:
   - Serve the Pineapple Upside-Down Cake warm or at room temperature, with a scoop of vanilla ice cream or a dollop of whipped cream if desired. Enjoy the sweet and fruity flavors of this classic dessert!

Mississippi Mud Pie

Ingredients:

For the crust:

- 1 1/2 cups chocolate cookie crumbs (about 20 cookies)
- 6 tablespoons unsalted butter, melted

For the filling:

- 1 cup heavy cream
- 1 1/2 cups semisweet chocolate chips
- 2 tablespoons unsalted butter
- 1 teaspoon vanilla extract

For the topping:

- 1 cup chopped pecans
- 2 cups miniature marshmallows

Instructions:

1. Preheat Oven:
    - Preheat your oven to 350°F (175°C).
2. Make the Crust:
    - In a mixing bowl, combine the chocolate cookie crumbs and melted butter. Mix until the crumbs are evenly moistened.
    - Press the mixture firmly into the bottom and up the sides of a 9-inch pie dish.
    - Bake the crust in the preheated oven for 10 minutes. Remove from the oven and let it cool completely.
3. Make the Filling:
    - In a saucepan, heat the heavy cream over medium heat until it just begins to simmer.
    - Remove the saucepan from the heat and stir in the chocolate chips, unsalted butter, and vanilla extract until smooth and creamy.

- Pour the chocolate filling into the cooled crust and spread it out evenly. Place the pie dish in the refrigerator to chill for about 30 minutes, or until the filling is set.
4. Add the Topping:
    - Once the filling is set, sprinkle the chopped pecans evenly over the top.
    - Arrange the miniature marshmallows on top of the pecans in an even layer.
5. Toast the Topping:
    - Preheat your broiler to high.
    - Place the pie dish under the broiler for 1-2 minutes, or until the marshmallows are golden brown and toasted. Watch closely to prevent burning.
    - Remove the pie from the oven and let it cool slightly before serving.
6. Serve:
    - Slice the Mississippi Mud Pie and serve it warm or chilled, depending on your preference.
    - Enjoy the rich and indulgent flavors of chocolate, pecans, and marshmallows in every bite!

Black Forest Cake

Ingredients:

For the chocolate cake:

- 1 3/4 cups all-purpose flour
- 3/4 cup unsweetened cocoa powder
- 2 cups granulated sugar
- 2 teaspoons baking powder
- 1 1/2 teaspoons baking soda
- 1 teaspoon salt
- 2 large eggs
- 1 cup whole milk
- 1/2 cup vegetable oil
- 2 teaspoons vanilla extract
- 1 cup boiling water

For the cherry filling:

- 24 ounces (about 4 cups) pitted cherries, fresh or canned, drained
- 1/4 cup granulated sugar
- 2 tablespoons cornstarch
- 1 tablespoon lemon juice

For the whipped cream frosting:

- 3 cups heavy cream, chilled
- 1/2 cup powdered sugar
- 2 teaspoons vanilla extract

For garnish:

- Chocolate shavings or curls
- Maraschino cherries

Instructions:

1. Preheat Oven and Prepare Pans:

- Preheat your oven to 350°F (175°C). Grease and flour two 9-inch round cake pans.
2. Make the Chocolate Cake:
    - In a large mixing bowl, sift together the flour, cocoa powder, sugar, baking powder, baking soda, and salt.
    - Add the eggs, milk, vegetable oil, and vanilla extract to the dry ingredients. Beat on medium speed for 2 minutes.
    - Stir in the boiling water until the batter is well combined (it will be thin).
    - Pour the batter evenly into the prepared cake pans.
    - Bake in the preheated oven for 30-35 minutes, or until a toothpick inserted into the center of the cakes comes out clean.
    - Remove the cakes from the oven and let them cool in the pans for 10 minutes before transferring them to wire racks to cool completely.
3. Make the Cherry Filling:
    - In a saucepan, combine the pitted cherries, granulated sugar, cornstarch, and lemon juice.
    - Cook over medium heat, stirring constantly, until the mixture thickens and comes to a simmer. Remove from heat and let it cool completely.
4. Make the Whipped Cream Frosting:
    - In a chilled mixing bowl, beat the heavy cream, powdered sugar, and vanilla extract until stiff peaks form.
5. Assemble the Cake:
    - Place one cooled chocolate cake layer on a serving plate. Spread half of the cherry filling over the top.
    - Spread a layer of whipped cream frosting over the cherry filling.
    - Place the second chocolate cake layer on top and repeat the process with the remaining cherry filling and whipped cream frosting.
    - Use the remaining whipped cream frosting to frost the top and sides of the cake.
6. Garnish:
    - Garnish the Black Forest Cake with chocolate shavings or curls and maraschino cherries.
7. Chill and Serve:
    - Refrigerate the cake for at least 1 hour before serving to allow the flavors to meld and the frosting to set.
    - Slice and serve the Black Forest Cake, and enjoy the rich chocolatey layers with the tart cherries and fluffy whipped cream!

Coconut Cream Pie

Ingredients:

For the pie crust:

- 1 1/4 cups all-purpose flour
- 1/2 teaspoon salt
- 1/2 teaspoon granulated sugar
- 1/2 cup (1 stick) cold unsalted butter, cut into small pieces
- 3-4 tablespoons ice water

For the coconut filling:

- 1 cup sweetened shredded coconut
- 2 cups whole milk
- 1/2 cup granulated sugar
- 1/4 cup cornstarch
- 4 large egg yolks
- 2 tablespoons unsalted butter
- 1 teaspoon vanilla extract

For the whipped cream topping:

- 1 cup heavy cream, chilled
- 2 tablespoons powdered sugar
- 1/2 teaspoon vanilla extract
- Toasted coconut flakes, for garnish (optional)

Instructions:

1. Make the Pie Crust:
    - In a large mixing bowl, combine the flour, salt, and granulated sugar. Add the cold butter pieces and use a pastry cutter or your fingers to work the butter into the flour mixture until it resembles coarse crumbs.
    - Gradually add the ice water, 1 tablespoon at a time, mixing until the dough just comes together and forms a ball.

- Shape the dough into a disk, wrap it tightly in plastic wrap, and refrigerate for at least 30 minutes.
2. Preheat Oven:
    - Preheat your oven to 375°F (190°C).
3. Roll Out the Crust:
    - On a lightly floured surface, roll out the chilled dough into a circle about 12 inches in diameter. Carefully transfer the dough to a 9-inch pie dish and press it gently into the bottom and up the sides. Trim any excess dough and crimp the edges as desired.
4. Blind Bake the Crust:
    - Line the pie crust with parchment paper or aluminum foil and fill it with pie weights or dried beans.
    - Bake in the preheated oven for 15 minutes. Remove the pie weights and parchment paper, and bake for an additional 10-15 minutes, or until the crust is golden brown. Remove from the oven and let it cool completely.
5. Make the Coconut Filling:
    - In a saucepan, heat the whole milk over medium heat until steaming but not boiling. Stir in the sweetened shredded coconut and let it steep for 15-20 minutes.
    - In a separate mixing bowl, whisk together the granulated sugar, cornstarch, and egg yolks until well combined.
    - Gradually whisk the hot milk and coconut mixture into the egg mixture.
    - Return the mixture to the saucepan and cook over medium heat, stirring constantly, until thickened.
    - Remove from heat and stir in the unsalted butter and vanilla extract until smooth. Let the filling cool slightly.
6. Assemble the Pie:
    - Pour the coconut filling into the cooled pie crust, spreading it out evenly.
7. Make the Whipped Cream Topping:
    - In a chilled mixing bowl, beat the heavy cream, powdered sugar, and vanilla extract until stiff peaks form.
    - Spread the whipped cream over the coconut filling.
8. Garnish:
    - Garnish the Coconut Cream Pie with toasted coconut flakes, if desired.
9. Chill and Serve:
    - Refrigerate the pie for at least 2-3 hours, or until the filling is set and the whipped cream is firm.
    - Slice and serve the Coconut Cream Pie, and enjoy the creamy coconut filling and fluffy whipped cream topping!

S'mores Bars

Ingredients:

- 2 cups graham cracker crumbs (about 14-16 whole graham crackers)
- 1/2 cup unsalted butter, melted
- 1/4 cup granulated sugar
- 1/2 teaspoon salt

For the chocolate layer:

- 2 cups semisweet chocolate chips
- 1 can (14 ounces) sweetened condensed milk

For the marshmallow layer:

- 3 cups mini marshmallows

Instructions:

1. Preheat Oven and Prepare Pan:
    - Preheat your oven to 350°F (175°C). Grease or line a 9x9-inch baking pan with parchment paper.
2. Make the Graham Cracker Crust:
    - In a mixing bowl, combine the graham cracker crumbs, melted butter, granulated sugar, and salt. Stir until the crumbs are evenly moistened.
    - Press the mixture firmly into the bottom of the prepared baking pan to form an even layer.
3. Bake the Crust:
    - Bake the crust in the preheated oven for 10 minutes. Remove from the oven and let it cool slightly.
4. Make the Chocolate Layer:
    - In a saucepan or microwave-safe bowl, melt the semisweet chocolate chips and sweetened condensed milk together, stirring until smooth and well combined.
    - Pour the chocolate mixture over the cooled graham cracker crust, spreading it out evenly with a spatula.

5. Add the Marshmallow Layer:
   - Sprinkle the mini marshmallows evenly over the chocolate layer, pressing them lightly into the chocolate.
6. Bake Again:
   - Return the pan to the oven and bake for an additional 10-12 minutes, or until the marshmallows are puffed and lightly golden brown.
7. Cool and Slice:
   - Remove the pan from the oven and let the S'mores Bars cool completely in the pan on a wire rack.
8. Chill and Serve:
   - Once cooled, transfer the pan to the refrigerator and chill for at least 1 hour to firm up the chocolate and marshmallow layers.
   - Once chilled, slice the S'mores Bars into squares or rectangles using a sharp knife.
   - Serve and enjoy the irresistible combination of graham crackers, chocolate, and marshmallows in these delightful S'mores Bars!

Oatmeal Raisin Cookies

Ingredients:

- 1 cup (2 sticks) unsalted butter, softened
- 1 cup packed brown sugar
- 1/2 cup granulated sugar
- 2 large eggs
- 1 teaspoon vanilla extract
- 1 1/2 cups all-purpose flour
- 1 teaspoon baking soda
- 1 teaspoon ground cinnamon
- 1/2 teaspoon salt
- 3 cups old-fashioned rolled oats
- 1 cup raisins

Instructions:

1. Preheat Oven:
    - Preheat your oven to 350°F (175°C). Line baking sheets with parchment paper or silicone baking mats.
2. Cream Butter and Sugars:
    - In a large mixing bowl, cream together the softened butter, brown sugar, and granulated sugar until light and fluffy.
3. Add Eggs and Vanilla:
    - Beat in the eggs one at a time, then stir in the vanilla extract until well combined.
4. Combine Dry Ingredients:
    - In a separate bowl, whisk together the flour, baking soda, ground cinnamon, and salt.
5. Combine Wet and Dry Ingredients:
    - Gradually add the dry ingredients to the wet ingredients, mixing until just combined.
6. Add Oats and Raisins:
    - Stir in the rolled oats and raisins until evenly distributed throughout the cookie dough.
7. Form Cookie Dough Balls:

- Drop rounded tablespoons of dough onto the prepared baking sheets, spacing them about 2 inches apart.
8. Bake:
    - Bake in the preheated oven for 10-12 minutes, or until the cookies are golden brown around the edges.
9. Cool and Serve:
    - Remove the cookies from the oven and let them cool on the baking sheets for a few minutes before transferring them to wire racks to cool completely.
    - Once cooled, serve and enjoy these delicious homemade Oatmeal Raisin Cookies with a glass of milk or your favorite hot beverage!

Peach Cobbler

Ingredients:

For the peach filling:

- 6 cups fresh or canned sliced peaches (about 6-8 peaches)
- 1/2 cup granulated sugar
- 1/4 cup brown sugar
- 1 tablespoon lemon juice
- 1 teaspoon vanilla extract
- 1/2 teaspoon ground cinnamon
- 1/4 teaspoon ground nutmeg
- 2 tablespoons cornstarch

For the cobbler topping:

- 1 1/2 cups all-purpose flour
- 1/2 cup granulated sugar
- 2 teaspoons baking powder
- 1/2 teaspoon salt
- 1/2 cup (1 stick) unsalted butter, melted
- 1/2 cup whole milk
- 1 teaspoon vanilla extract

Instructions:

1. Preheat Oven:
    - Preheat your oven to 375°F (190°C). Grease a 9x13-inch baking dish or a similar-sized baking dish.
2. Prepare Peach Filling:
    - In a large mixing bowl, combine the sliced peaches, granulated sugar, brown sugar, lemon juice, vanilla extract, ground cinnamon, ground nutmeg, and cornstarch. Stir until the peaches are evenly coated. Transfer the mixture to the prepared baking dish, spreading it out evenly.
3. Make Cobbler Topping:

- In another mixing bowl, whisk together the all-purpose flour, granulated sugar, baking powder, and salt.
- Add the melted butter, whole milk, and vanilla extract to the dry ingredients, and stir until just combined. The batter will be thick and slightly lumpy.

4. Assemble and Bake:
   - Drop spoonfuls of the cobbler batter evenly over the top of the peach filling in the baking dish, covering it as much as possible.
   - Place the baking dish in the preheated oven and bake for 40-45 minutes, or until the cobbler topping is golden brown and the peach filling is bubbling around the edges.

5. Serve:
   - Remove the peach cobbler from the oven and let it cool slightly before serving.
   - Serve warm with a scoop of vanilla ice cream or a dollop of whipped cream, if desired.
   - Enjoy the delicious flavors of ripe peaches and buttery cobbler topping in this classic Peach Cobbler recipe!

Pumpkin Pie

Ingredients:

For the pie crust:

- 1 1/4 cups all-purpose flour
- 1/2 teaspoon salt
- 1/2 teaspoon granulated sugar
- 1/2 cup (1 stick) cold unsalted butter, cut into small pieces
- 3-4 tablespoons ice water

For the pumpkin filling:

- 1 can (15 ounces) pumpkin puree (not pumpkin pie filling)
- 3/4 cup packed light brown sugar
- 2 large eggs
- 1 cup evaporated milk
- 1 teaspoon vanilla extract
- 1 teaspoon ground cinnamon
- 1/2 teaspoon ground ginger
- 1/4 teaspoon ground cloves
- 1/4 teaspoon ground nutmeg
- 1/2 teaspoon salt

Instructions:

1. Make the Pie Crust:
    - In a large mixing bowl, combine the flour, salt, and granulated sugar. Add the cold butter pieces and use a pastry cutter or your fingers to work the butter into the flour mixture until it resembles coarse crumbs.
    - Gradually add the ice water, 1 tablespoon at a time, mixing until the dough just comes together and forms a ball.
    - Shape the dough into a disk, wrap it tightly in plastic wrap, and refrigerate for at least 30 minutes.
2. Preheat Oven:
    - Preheat your oven to 425°F (220°C).

3. Roll Out the Crust:
   - On a lightly floured surface, roll out the chilled dough into a circle about 12 inches in diameter. Carefully transfer the dough to a 9-inch pie dish and press it gently into the bottom and up the sides. Trim any excess dough and crimp the edges as desired.
4. Make the Pumpkin Filling:
   - In a large mixing bowl, whisk together the pumpkin puree, packed light brown sugar, eggs, evaporated milk, vanilla extract, ground cinnamon, ground ginger, ground cloves, ground nutmeg, and salt until smooth and well combined.
5. Pour Filling Into Crust:
   - Pour the pumpkin filling into the prepared pie crust, spreading it out evenly.
6. Bake:
   - Place the pie on a baking sheet and bake in the preheated oven for 15 minutes.
   - Reduce the oven temperature to 350°F (175°C) and continue baking for 40-50 minutes, or until the filling is set and the crust is golden brown.
   - If the edges of the crust begin to brown too quickly, you can cover them with aluminum foil.
7. Cool and Serve:
   - Remove the pie from the oven and let it cool completely on a wire rack before serving.
   - Slice and serve the Pumpkin Pie, and enjoy the rich, creamy pumpkin filling and flaky pie crust!

Snickerdoodles

Ingredients:

For the cookie dough:

- 2 3/4 cups all-purpose flour
- 2 teaspoons cream of tartar
- 1 teaspoon baking soda
- 1/4 teaspoon salt
- 1 cup (2 sticks) unsalted butter, softened
- 1 1/2 cups granulated sugar
- 2 large eggs
- 1 teaspoon vanilla extract

For the cinnamon-sugar coating:

- 1/4 cup granulated sugar
- 2 tablespoons ground cinnamon

Instructions:

1. Preheat Oven:
    - Preheat your oven to 375°F (190°C). Line baking sheets with parchment paper or silicone baking mats.
2. Make the Cookie Dough:
    - In a medium mixing bowl, whisk together the all-purpose flour, cream of tartar, baking soda, and salt. Set aside.
    - In a large mixing bowl, cream together the softened butter and granulated sugar until light and fluffy.
    - Beat in the eggs one at a time, then stir in the vanilla extract until well combined.
    - Gradually add the dry ingredients to the wet ingredients, mixing until just combined. Do not overmix.
3. Prepare the Cinnamon-Sugar Coating:
    - In a small bowl, combine the granulated sugar and ground cinnamon.
4. Form Cookie Dough Balls:
    - Shape the cookie dough into 1-inch balls using a cookie scoop or your hands.

- Roll each dough ball in the cinnamon-sugar mixture until evenly coated.
5. Place on Baking Sheets:
    - Place the coated dough balls onto the prepared baking sheets, spacing them about 2 inches apart.
6. Bake:
    - Bake in the preheated oven for 8-10 minutes, or until the cookies are set and the edges are lightly golden brown.
7. Cool and Serve:
    - Remove the cookies from the oven and let them cool on the baking sheets for a few minutes before transferring them to wire racks to cool completely.
    - Once cooled, serve and enjoy these classic Snickerdoodles with a glass of milk or your favorite hot beverage!

Tiramisu

Ingredients:

- 6 large egg yolks
- 3/4 cup granulated sugar
- 1 cup mascarpone cheese, softened
- 1 1/2 cups heavy cream
- 1 cup strong brewed coffee, cooled to room temperature
- 2 tablespoons coffee liqueur (optional)
- 1 teaspoon vanilla extract
- 24-30 ladyfinger cookies (savoiardi)
- Unsweetened cocoa powder, for dusting

Instructions:

1. Prepare the Mascarpone Mixture:
    - In a large mixing bowl, whisk together the egg yolks and granulated sugar until thick and pale.
    - Add the softened mascarpone cheese to the egg mixture and beat until smooth and creamy.
2. Whip the Heavy Cream:
    - In a separate mixing bowl, whip the heavy cream until stiff peaks form.
    - Gently fold the whipped cream into the mascarpone mixture until well combined. Set aside.
3. Prepare the Coffee Soaking Mixture:
    - In a shallow dish, combine the cooled brewed coffee and coffee liqueur (if using). Stir in the vanilla extract.
4. Assemble the Tiramisu:
    - Quickly dip each ladyfinger into the coffee mixture, making sure not to soak them too long or they will become soggy.
    - Arrange a layer of soaked ladyfingers in the bottom of a 9x13-inch dish or a similar-sized serving dish.
    - Spread half of the mascarpone mixture over the soaked ladyfingers, smoothing it out into an even layer.
    - Repeat with another layer of soaked ladyfingers and the remaining mascarpone mixture.
5. Chill the Tiramisu:

- Cover the assembled tiramisu with plastic wrap and refrigerate for at least 4 hours, or preferably overnight, to allow the flavors to meld and the dessert to set.
6. Dust with Cocoa Powder:
    - Just before serving, remove the tiramisu from the refrigerator and dust the top generously with unsweetened cocoa powder using a fine-mesh sieve.
7. Slice and Serve:
    - Use a sharp knife to slice the tiramisu into squares or rectangles.
    - Serve chilled and enjoy the rich, creamy, and coffee-flavored layers of this classic Italian dessert!

Cherry Pie

Ingredients:

For the pie crust:

- 2 1/2 cups all-purpose flour
- 1 teaspoon salt
- 1 tablespoon granulated sugar
- 1 cup (2 sticks) unsalted butter, cold and cut into small cubes
- 6-8 tablespoons ice water

For the cherry filling:

- 5 cups fresh or frozen cherries, pitted
- 1 cup granulated sugar
- 1/4 cup cornstarch
- 1 tablespoon lemon juice
- 1/2 teaspoon almond extract (optional)
- 1/4 teaspoon ground cinnamon (optional)
- 1 tablespoon unsalted butter, cut into small pieces

Instructions:

1. Make the Pie Crust:
    - In a large mixing bowl, combine the all-purpose flour, salt, and granulated sugar. Add the cold cubed butter.
    - Use a pastry cutter or your fingers to work the butter into the flour mixture until it resembles coarse crumbs with some pea-sized pieces of butter remaining.
    - Gradually add the ice water, 1 tablespoon at a time, mixing with a fork, until the dough starts to come together.
    - Gather the dough into a ball, divide it in half, and flatten each half into a disk. Wrap each disk tightly in plastic wrap and refrigerate for at least 1 hour.
2. Prepare the Cherry Filling:

- In a large mixing bowl, combine the pitted cherries, granulated sugar, cornstarch, lemon juice, almond extract (if using), and ground cinnamon (if using). Toss until the cherries are well coated.
- Let the cherry filling sit at room temperature while you prepare the pie crust.

3. Preheat Oven:
   - Preheat your oven to 400°F (200°C).
4. Roll Out the Crust:
   - On a lightly floured surface, roll out one of the chilled pie crust disks into a circle about 12 inches in diameter. Carefully transfer it to a 9-inch pie dish, pressing it gently into the bottom and up the sides.
5. Add the Cherry Filling:
   - Pour the cherry filling into the prepared pie crust, spreading it out evenly. Dot the top of the filling with small pieces of unsalted butter.
6. Roll Out the Top Crust:
   - Roll out the second chilled pie crust disk into a circle about 12 inches in diameter. You can either place the entire crust over the filling and cut slits for ventilation, or cut the crust into strips for a lattice design.
7. Seal and Crimp the Edges:
   - If using a full top crust, place it over the filling and trim any excess dough, then crimp the edges to seal. If using a lattice design, weave the strips over the filling and trim any excess dough, then crimp the edges to seal.
8. Bake:
   - Place the pie on a baking sheet to catch any drips and bake in the preheated oven for 45-55 minutes, or until the crust is golden brown and the filling is bubbly.
9. Cool and Serve:
   - Remove the pie from the oven and let it cool on a wire rack for at least 2 hours before serving to allow the filling to set.
   - Serve slices of cherry pie warm or at room temperature, optionally topped with a scoop of vanilla ice cream or a dollop of whipped cream. Enjoy the delicious flavors of sweet cherries encased in a flaky crust!

Chocolate Mousse

Ingredients:

- 8 ounces (about 225g) semisweet or bittersweet chocolate, chopped
- 2 cups heavy cream, divided
- 1/4 cup granulated sugar
- 4 large egg yolks
- 1 teaspoon vanilla extract

Optional Garnishes:

- Whipped cream
- Chocolate shavings or curls
- Fresh berries

Instructions:

1. Melt the Chocolate:
    - Place the chopped chocolate in a heatproof bowl set over a saucepan of simmering water. Stir the chocolate occasionally until melted and smooth. Remove from heat and let it cool slightly.
2. Whip the Cream:
    - In a separate mixing bowl, whip 1 1/2 cups of heavy cream with an electric mixer on medium-high speed until soft peaks form.
    - Add the granulated sugar and continue to whip until stiff peaks form. Be careful not to overwhip.
3. Mix in the Egg Yolks:
    - In a small bowl, whisk the egg yolks until smooth. Gradually whisk in a small amount of the whipped cream to temper the yolks.
4. Combine the Chocolate and Egg Yolk Mixture:
    - Gradually pour the melted chocolate into the egg yolk mixture, whisking constantly until smooth and well combined.
5. Fold in the Whipped Cream:
    - Gently fold the remaining whipped cream into the chocolate mixture until no streaks remain. Use a rubber spatula and gently fold from the bottom of the bowl, lifting the mixture over the top until fully incorporated.
6. Chill the Mousse:

- Divide the chocolate mousse among serving dishes or glasses. Cover and refrigerate for at least 2 hours, or until set.

7. Serve and Garnish:
    - Before serving, whip the remaining 1/2 cup of heavy cream until soft peaks form. Dollop or pipe whipped cream onto each serving of chocolate mousse.
    - Garnish with chocolate shavings or curls and fresh berries, if desired.

8. Enjoy!
    - Serve the chocolate mousse chilled and enjoy its rich, creamy texture and decadent chocolate flavor!

Whoopie Pies

Ingredients:

For the cookies:

- 2 cups all-purpose flour
- 1/2 cup unsweetened cocoa powder
- 1 teaspoon baking soda
- 1/2 teaspoon salt
- 1/2 cup unsalted butter, softened
- 1 cup granulated sugar
- 1 large egg
- 1 teaspoon vanilla extract
- 1 cup buttermilk

For the filling:

- 1/2 cup unsalted butter, softened
- 1 cup powdered sugar
- 1 teaspoon vanilla extract
- 1 1/2 cups marshmallow fluff

Instructions:

1. Preheat Oven:
    - Preheat your oven to 350°F (175°C). Line baking sheets with parchment paper or silicone baking mats.
2. Make the Cookies:
    - In a medium mixing bowl, whisk together the flour, cocoa powder, baking soda, and salt. Set aside.
    - In a large mixing bowl, cream together the softened butter and granulated sugar until light and fluffy.
    - Beat in the egg and vanilla extract until well combined.
    - Gradually add the dry ingredients to the wet ingredients, alternating with the buttermilk, beginning and ending with the dry ingredients. Mix until just combined.
3. Form Cookies:

- Drop rounded tablespoons of cookie dough onto the prepared baking sheets, spacing them about 2 inches apart.
4. Bake:
    - Bake in the preheated oven for 10-12 minutes, or until the cookies are set and slightly firm to the touch.
    - Remove from the oven and let the cookies cool on the baking sheets for a few minutes before transferring them to wire racks to cool completely.
5. Make the Filling:
    - In a medium mixing bowl, beat together the softened butter, powdered sugar, and vanilla extract until smooth and creamy.
    - Add the marshmallow fluff and beat until well combined and fluffy.
6. Assemble the Whoopie Pies:
    - Once the cookies are completely cooled, spread a generous amount of filling onto the flat side of one cookie.
    - Top with another cookie, flat side down, to form a sandwich.
    - Repeat with the remaining cookies and filling.
7. Serve and Enjoy:
    - Serve the Whoopie Pies immediately, or store them in an airtight container in the refrigerator for up to 3 days.
    - Enjoy the soft, cake-like cookies filled with fluffy marshmallow filling in these delicious Whoopie Pies!

Cinnamon Rolls

Ingredients:

For the dough:

- 1 cup warm milk (about 110°F)
- 2 1/4 teaspoons (1 packet) active dry yeast
- 1/2 cup granulated sugar
- 1/3 cup unsalted butter, melted
- 2 large eggs
- 1 teaspoon salt
- 4 1/2 to 5 cups all-purpose flour

For the filling:

- 1/2 cup unsalted butter, softened
- 1 cup packed brown sugar
- 2 tablespoons ground cinnamon

For the cream cheese frosting:

- 1/4 cup unsalted butter, softened
- 4 ounces cream cheese, softened
- 1 1/2 cups powdered sugar
- 1/2 teaspoon vanilla extract
- Pinch of salt

Instructions:

1. Activate the Yeast:
    - In a small bowl, combine the warm milk and yeast. Let it sit for about 5-10 minutes until frothy.
2. Make the Dough:
    - In a large mixing bowl, combine the yeast mixture with the sugar, melted butter, eggs, and salt.
    - Gradually add 4 1/2 cups of flour, mixing until the dough comes together.

- Turn the dough out onto a floured surface and knead for about 5-7 minutes, adding more flour as needed, until the dough is smooth and elastic.

3. First Rise:
   - Place the dough in a greased bowl, cover it with a clean kitchen towel, and let it rise in a warm place for about 1-1 1/2 hours, or until doubled in size.
4. Make the Filling:
   - In a small bowl, mix together the softened butter, brown sugar, and ground cinnamon until well combined.
5. Roll out the Dough:
   - Punch down the risen dough and roll it out on a floured surface into a rectangle, about 16x12 inches.
6. Add the Filling:
   - Spread the filling mixture evenly over the rolled-out dough, leaving about a 1/2-inch border around the edges.
7. Roll up the Dough:
   - Starting from the long side, tightly roll up the dough into a log.
8. Cut into Rolls:
   - Use a sharp knife to slice the dough into 12 equal-sized rolls.
9. Second Rise:
   - Place the rolls in a greased baking dish, cover them with a kitchen towel, and let them rise for another 30-45 minutes, or until doubled in size.
10. Bake:
    - Preheat your oven to 350°F (175°C).
    - Once risen, bake the cinnamon rolls in the preheated oven for 20-25 minutes, or until golden brown.
11. Make the Frosting:
    - While the rolls are baking, prepare the cream cheese frosting. In a mixing bowl, beat together the softened butter and cream cheese until smooth.
    - Add the powdered sugar, vanilla extract, and a pinch of salt, and beat until creamy and well combined.
12. Frost the Rolls:
    - Once the cinnamon rolls are done baking, let them cool for a few minutes, then spread the cream cheese frosting over the warm rolls.
13. Serve and Enjoy:
    - Serve the cinnamon rolls warm and enjoy the gooey, sweet goodness!

Bread Pudding

Ingredients:

- 6 cups stale bread, torn into bite-sized pieces (such as French bread or brioche)
- 2 cups whole milk
- 1 cup heavy cream
- 4 large eggs
- 1 cup granulated sugar
- 1 teaspoon vanilla extract
- 1/2 teaspoon ground cinnamon
- 1/4 teaspoon ground nutmeg
- 1/4 teaspoon salt
- 1/2 cup raisins or other dried fruit (optional)
- Butter or cooking spray, for greasing the baking dish

Optional Sauce:

- 1/2 cup unsalted butter
- 1 cup packed brown sugar
- 1/2 cup heavy cream
- 1 teaspoon vanilla extract
- Pinch of salt

Instructions:

1. Preheat Oven:
    - Preheat your oven to 350°F (175°C). Grease a 9x13-inch baking dish with butter or cooking spray.
2. Prepare the Bread:
    - Place the torn bread pieces in the prepared baking dish, spreading them out evenly.
3. Make the Custard Mixture:
    - In a large mixing bowl, whisk together the whole milk, heavy cream, eggs, granulated sugar, vanilla extract, ground cinnamon, ground nutmeg, and salt until well combined.
    - If using, stir in the raisins or other dried fruit.
4. Pour Over Bread:

- Pour the custard mixture evenly over the bread pieces in the baking dish, pressing down gently to ensure all the bread is soaked in the mixture.

5. Bake:
    - Place the baking dish in the preheated oven and bake for 45-50 minutes, or until the bread pudding is set and golden brown on top. The center should be slightly firm to the touch.

6. Make the Optional Sauce (if desired):
    - In a saucepan over medium heat, melt the unsalted butter.
    - Stir in the brown sugar and heavy cream, whisking constantly until the sugar is dissolved and the mixture is smooth.
    - Remove from heat and stir in the vanilla extract and a pinch of salt.

7. Serve:
    - Serve the warm bread pudding drizzled with the optional sauce, if desired.
    - Bread pudding can also be served with whipped cream, vanilla ice cream, or a dusting of powdered sugar.
    - Enjoy the cozy comfort of this classic dessert!

Angel Food Cake

Ingredients:

- 1 cup cake flour
- 1 1/2 cups granulated sugar, divided
- 12 large egg whites, at room temperature
- 1 teaspoon cream of tartar
- 1/4 teaspoon salt
- 1 teaspoon vanilla extract
- 1/2 teaspoon almond extract (optional)
- Fresh berries, for serving (optional)
- Whipped cream, for serving (optional)

Instructions:

1. Preheat Oven and Prepare Pan:
    - Preheat your oven to 350°F (175°C). Ensure the oven rack is positioned in the lower third of the oven.
    - Do not grease the angel food cake pan. It needs to be clean and dry to allow the cake to cling to the sides as it rises.
2. Sift Flour and Sugar:
    - In a bowl, sift together the cake flour and 3/4 cup of granulated sugar. Set aside.
3. Whip Egg Whites:
    - In a large mixing bowl, beat the egg whites with an electric mixer on medium speed until frothy.
    - Add cream of tartar and salt. Increase speed to medium-high and continue to beat until soft peaks form.
    - Gradually add the remaining 3/4 cup of granulated sugar, about 2 tablespoons at a time, while continuing to beat until stiff peaks form.
    - Stir in vanilla extract and almond extract (if using) until well combined.
4. Fold in Flour Mixture:
    - Gently fold the sifted flour mixture into the whipped egg whites in three additions, being careful not to deflate the mixture.
    - Fold until no streaks of flour remain.
5. Transfer Batter to Pan:
    - Carefully transfer the batter to an ungreased angel food cake pan. Use a spatula to evenly distribute the batter and smooth the top.

6. Bake:
   - Bake in the preheated oven for 35-40 minutes, or until the top is golden brown and the cake springs back when lightly touched.
   - The cake should also start to pull away from the sides of the pan.
7. Cool:
   - Once baked, immediately invert the pan onto a cooling rack. If your pan has feet, simply flip it over. If not, you can balance it on the neck of a bottle.
   - Let the cake cool completely in the inverted position. This helps prevent it from collapsing.
8. Remove from Pan:
   - Once the cake is completely cooled, run a knife around the edges of the pan and remove the cake from the pan.
9. Serve:
   - Slice the angel food cake using a serrated knife.
   - Serve slices of angel food cake with fresh berries and whipped cream, if desired.
   - Enjoy the light and fluffy texture of this classic cake!

Ice Cream Sandwiches

Ingredients:

For the cookies:

- 1 cup (2 sticks) unsalted butter, softened
- 1 cup granulated sugar
- 1 cup brown sugar, packed
- 2 large eggs
- 2 teaspoons vanilla extract
- 2 1/4 cups all-purpose flour
- 1 teaspoon baking soda
- 1/2 teaspoon salt
- 1 cup semisweet chocolate chips

For assembly:

- Ice cream of your choice (vanilla, chocolate, strawberry, etc.)
- Optional toppings (sprinkles, crushed nuts, mini chocolate chips, etc.)

Instructions:

1. Preheat Oven:
    - Preheat your oven to 375°F (190°C). Line baking sheets with parchment paper or silicone baking mats.
2. Make the Cookie Dough:
    - In a large mixing bowl, cream together the softened butter, granulated sugar, and brown sugar until light and fluffy.
    - Beat in the eggs one at a time, then stir in the vanilla extract.
3. Combine Dry Ingredients:
    - In a separate bowl, whisk together the all-purpose flour, baking soda, and salt.
4. Mix Wet and Dry Ingredients:
    - Gradually add the dry ingredients to the wet ingredients, mixing until just combined.
    - Stir in the semisweet chocolate chips until evenly distributed throughout the cookie dough.
5. Form Cookie Dough Balls:

- Drop rounded tablespoons of cookie dough onto the prepared baking sheets, spacing them about 2 inches apart.
- Flatten each dough ball slightly with your fingers or the back of a spoon.

6. Bake:
   - Bake in the preheated oven for 8-10 minutes, or until the cookies are set and lightly golden brown around the edges.
   - Remove from the oven and let the cookies cool on the baking sheets for a few minutes before transferring them to wire racks to cool completely.

7. Assemble the Ice Cream Sandwiches:
   - Once the cookies are completely cooled, place a scoop of ice cream (about 1/4 cup) onto the flat side of one cookie.
   - Top with another cookie, flat side down, to form a sandwich.
   - Optionally, roll the edges of the ice cream sandwich in toppings like sprinkles, crushed nuts, or mini chocolate chips.

8. Freeze:
   - Place the assembled ice cream sandwiches on a baking sheet lined with parchment paper and freeze for at least 1-2 hours, or until the ice cream is firm.

9. Serve and Enjoy:
   - Serve the frozen ice cream sandwiches and enjoy this nostalgic treat!
   - Store any leftover ice cream sandwiches in an airtight container in the freezer for future enjoyment.

Apple Crisp

Ingredients:

For the filling:

- 6 cups peeled, cored, and sliced apples (such as Granny Smith or Honeycrisp)
- 1/4 cup granulated sugar
- 2 tablespoons all-purpose flour
- 1 teaspoon ground cinnamon
- 1/4 teaspoon ground nutmeg
- 1 tablespoon lemon juice

For the topping:

- 1 cup old-fashioned rolled oats
- 1/2 cup all-purpose flour
- 1/2 cup packed brown sugar
- 1/2 teaspoon ground cinnamon
- 1/4 teaspoon salt
- 1/2 cup (1 stick) unsalted butter, cold and cut into small pieces

Instructions:

1. Preheat Oven:
   - Preheat your oven to 350°F (175°C). Grease a 9x13-inch baking dish or a similar-sized baking dish.
2. Prepare the Apple Filling:
   - In a large mixing bowl, toss the sliced apples with granulated sugar, all-purpose flour, ground cinnamon, ground nutmeg, and lemon juice until the apples are evenly coated. Transfer the apple mixture to the prepared baking dish, spreading it out evenly.
3. Make the Crisp Topping:
   - In a separate mixing bowl, combine the old-fashioned rolled oats, all-purpose flour, packed brown sugar, ground cinnamon, and salt.

- Add the cold, diced unsalted butter to the dry ingredients. Use a pastry cutter or your fingers to work the butter into the mixture until it resembles coarse crumbs with some larger pea-sized pieces.
4. Assemble and Bake:
    - Sprinkle the crisp topping evenly over the apple filling in the baking dish, covering it as much as possible.
    - Place the baking dish in the preheated oven and bake for 40-45 minutes, or until the topping is golden brown and the apple filling is bubbly around the edges.
5. Cool and Serve:
    - Remove the apple crisp from the oven and let it cool slightly before serving.
    - Serve warm with a scoop of vanilla ice cream or a dollop of whipped cream, if desired.
    - Enjoy the warm, comforting flavors of cinnamon-spiced apples and crunchy oat topping in this delicious Apple Crisp!

Raspberry Cheesecake Bars

Ingredients:

For the crust:

- 1 1/2 cups graham cracker crumbs
- 1/4 cup granulated sugar
- 1/2 cup (1 stick) unsalted butter, melted

For the cheesecake filling:

- 16 ounces (2 packages) cream cheese, softened
- 2/3 cup granulated sugar
- 2 large eggs
- 1 teaspoon vanilla extract
- 1/4 cup sour cream or Greek yogurt

For the raspberry swirl:

- 1 cup fresh or frozen raspberries
- 2 tablespoons granulated sugar
- 1 tablespoon water
- 1 teaspoon cornstarch

Instructions:

1. Preheat Oven:
    - Preheat your oven to 325°F (160°C). Line an 8x8-inch baking dish with parchment paper, leaving some overhang on the sides for easy removal.
2. Make the Crust:
    - In a mixing bowl, combine the graham cracker crumbs, granulated sugar, and melted butter. Mix until well combined.
    - Press the mixture firmly and evenly into the bottom of the prepared baking dish.
3. Prepare the Raspberry Swirl:
    - In a small saucepan, combine the raspberries, granulated sugar, water, and cornstarch. Cook over medium heat, stirring occasionally, until the raspberries break down and the mixture thickens, about 5-7 minutes.

- Remove from heat and strain the mixture through a fine-mesh sieve to remove the seeds. Allow the raspberry sauce to cool slightly.
4. Make the Cheesecake Filling:
    - In a large mixing bowl, beat the softened cream cheese and granulated sugar with an electric mixer until smooth and creamy.
    - Add the eggs one at a time, beating well after each addition.
    - Mix in the vanilla extract and sour cream (or Greek yogurt) until well combined.
5. Assemble the Bars:
    - Pour the cheesecake filling over the prepared crust in the baking dish, spreading it out evenly.
    - Drizzle the raspberry sauce over the cheesecake filling in parallel lines.
    - Use a toothpick or skewer to create swirls by gently dragging it through the raspberry sauce and cheesecake filling.
6. Bake:
    - Place the baking dish in the preheated oven and bake for 35-40 minutes, or until the edges are set and the center is slightly jiggly.
7. Cool and Chill:
    - Remove the raspberry cheesecake bars from the oven and let them cool to room temperature in the baking dish.
    - Once cooled, refrigerate the bars for at least 4 hours, or preferably overnight, to allow them to set completely.
8. Slice and Serve:
    - Use the parchment paper overhang to lift the cheesecake bars out of the baking dish.
    - Cut the bars into squares using a sharp knife.
    - Serve chilled and enjoy the creamy cheesecake with a delightful raspberry swirl!

Blondies

Ingredients:

- 1 cup (2 sticks) unsalted butter, melted
- 2 cups packed light brown sugar
- 2 large eggs
- 1 tablespoon vanilla extract
- 2 cups all-purpose flour
- 1 teaspoon baking powder
- 1/2 teaspoon salt
- 1 cup semisweet chocolate chips (optional)
- 1 cup chopped nuts, such as walnuts or pecans (optional)

Instructions:

1. Preheat Oven:
    - Preheat your oven to 350°F (175°C). Grease or line a 9x13-inch baking dish with parchment paper, leaving some overhang on the sides for easy removal.
2. Mix Wet Ingredients:
    - In a large mixing bowl, whisk together the melted butter and packed light brown sugar until well combined and smooth.
    - Add the eggs and vanilla extract to the butter-sugar mixture and whisk until smooth.
3. Combine Dry Ingredients:
    - In a separate mixing bowl, sift together the all-purpose flour, baking powder, and salt.
4. Combine Wet and Dry Ingredients:
    - Gradually add the dry ingredients to the wet ingredients, stirring until just combined. Be careful not to overmix.
5. Add Optional Mix-Ins:
    - If desired, fold in the semisweet chocolate chips and chopped nuts until evenly distributed throughout the blondie batter.
6. Spread Batter in Baking Dish:
    - Transfer the blondie batter to the prepared baking dish, spreading it out evenly with a spatula or the back of a spoon.
7. Bake:

- Bake in the preheated oven for 25-30 minutes, or until the blondies are set and golden brown around the edges. A toothpick inserted into the center should come out clean or with a few moist crumbs.
8. Cool and Slice:
    - Remove the blondies from the oven and let them cool completely in the baking dish on a wire rack.
    - Once cooled, use a sharp knife to slice the blondies into squares or rectangles.
9. Serve and Enjoy:
    - Serve the blondies at room temperature or slightly warmed, as desired.
    - Store any leftover blondies in an airtight container at room temperature for up to 3 days, or in the refrigerator for longer freshness.

These blondies are wonderfully chewy, moist, and packed with sweet brown sugar flavor. Enjoy them as a delightful treat any time of day!

Lemon Meringue Pie

Ingredients:

For the crust:

- 1 1/4 cups all-purpose flour
- 1/2 teaspoon salt
- 1/3 cup cold unsalted butter, cut into small cubes
- 1/4 cup cold vegetable shortening, cut into small pieces
- 2-4 tablespoons ice water

For the lemon filling:

- 1 cup granulated sugar
- 1/4 cup cornstarch
- 1/4 teaspoon salt
- 1 1/2 cups water
- 4 large egg yolks, lightly beaten
- 1 tablespoon lemon zest
- 1/2 cup freshly squeezed lemon juice (about 3-4 lemons)
- 2 tablespoons unsalted butter

For the meringue:

- 4 large egg whites, at room temperature
- 1/4 teaspoon cream of tartar
- 1/2 cup granulated sugar

Instructions:

1. Prepare the Crust:
    - In a large mixing bowl, combine the all-purpose flour and salt.
    - Add the cold butter and vegetable shortening to the flour mixture. Use a pastry cutter or your fingers to work the fats into the flour until the mixture resembles coarse crumbs.
    - Gradually add the ice water, 1 tablespoon at a time, mixing with a fork, until the dough comes together.
    - Shape the dough into a disk, wrap it in plastic wrap, and refrigerate for at least 1 hour.

2. **Preheat Oven:**
   - Preheat your oven to 375°F (190°C).
3. **Roll out the Crust:**
   - On a lightly floured surface, roll out the chilled dough into a circle large enough to fit into a 9-inch pie dish.
   - Transfer the dough to the pie dish, pressing it gently into the bottom and up the sides. Trim any excess dough and crimp the edges decoratively.
4. **Par-Bake the Crust:**
   - Line the pie crust with parchment paper or aluminum foil and fill it with pie weights or dried beans.
   - Bake in the preheated oven for 15 minutes. Remove the weights and parchment paper, then bake for an additional 5-7 minutes, or until the crust is golden brown. Remove from the oven and set aside to cool.
5. **Prepare the Lemon Filling:**
   - In a medium saucepan, whisk together the granulated sugar, cornstarch, and salt.
   - Gradually whisk in the water until smooth. Cook over medium heat, stirring constantly, until the mixture thickens and comes to a boil.
   - Boil for 1 minute, then remove the saucepan from the heat.
   - Gradually whisk about 1/2 cup of the hot sugar mixture into the beaten egg yolks to temper them, then pour the egg yolk mixture back into the saucepan, whisking constantly.
   - Return the saucepan to the heat and bring the mixture to a gentle boil, stirring constantly. Boil for 1 minute.
   - Remove the saucepan from the heat and stir in the lemon zest, lemon juice, and unsalted butter until the butter is melted and the mixture is smooth.
6. **Assemble the Pie:**
   - Pour the hot lemon filling into the pre-baked pie crust, spreading it out evenly.
7. **Prepare the Meringue:**
   - In a clean mixing bowl, beat the egg whites and cream of tartar with an electric mixer on medium speed until soft peaks form.
   - Gradually add the granulated sugar, 1 tablespoon at a time, while continuing to beat on high speed until stiff peaks form and the sugar is dissolved.
8. **Top the Pie with Meringue:**
   - Spread the meringue over the hot lemon filling, making sure to spread it all the way to the edges of the crust to seal it in.

9. Bake the Pie:
   - Bake the pie in the preheated oven for 10-12 minutes, or until the meringue is golden brown.
10. Cool and Serve:
    - Remove the pie from the oven and let it cool completely on a wire rack.
    - Once cooled, refrigerate the pie for at least 4 hours, or until set.
    - Slice and serve the lemon meringue pie chilled, and enjoy its tangy lemon filling and fluffy meringue topping!

Fudge Brownies

Ingredients:

- 1 cup (225g) unsalted butter
- 2 cups (400g) granulated sugar
- 4 large eggs
- 1 teaspoon vanilla extract
- 1 cup (120g) unsweetened cocoa powder
- 1 cup (125g) all-purpose flour
- 1/2 teaspoon salt
- 1/2 teaspoon baking powder
- 1 cup (175g) semisweet chocolate chips (optional)

Instructions:

1. Preheat Oven:
    - Preheat your oven to 350°F (175°C). Grease a 9x13-inch baking pan or line it with parchment paper, leaving some overhang on the sides for easy removal.
2. Melt Butter:
    - In a medium saucepan, melt the butter over medium heat. Remove from heat once melted.
3. Mix Wet Ingredients:
    - In a large mixing bowl, whisk together the granulated sugar, eggs, and vanilla extract until well combined.
    - Gradually pour the melted butter into the sugar mixture, whisking continuously until smooth.
4. Combine Dry Ingredients:
    - In a separate bowl, sift together the cocoa powder, all-purpose flour, salt, and baking powder.
5. Mix Wet and Dry Ingredients:
    - Gradually add the dry ingredients to the wet ingredients, stirring until just combined. Be careful not to overmix.
    - If desired, fold in the semisweet chocolate chips until evenly distributed throughout the batter.
6. Bake:

- Pour the brownie batter into the prepared baking pan, spreading it out evenly with a spatula.
- Bake in the preheated oven for 25-30 minutes, or until a toothpick inserted into the center comes out with a few moist crumbs.
- Be careful not to overbake, as you want the brownies to be fudgy and moist.

7. Cool and Slice:
   - Allow the brownies to cool completely in the pan on a wire rack.
   - Once cooled, use a sharp knife to slice the brownies into squares or rectangles.
8. Serve and Enjoy:
   - Serve the fudge brownies at room temperature or slightly warmed, as desired.
   - Enjoy the rich, chocolatey goodness of these homemade brownies!

These brownies are perfect for satisfying your chocolate cravings and are sure to be a hit with family and friends!

Texas Sheet Cake

Ingredients:

For the cake:

- 2 cups (250g) all-purpose flour
- 2 cups (400g) granulated sugar
- 1 teaspoon baking soda
- 1/2 teaspoon salt
- 1 cup (240ml) water
- 1/2 cup (115g) unsalted butter
- 1/4 cup (20g) unsweetened cocoa powder
- 1/2 cup (120ml) buttermilk
- 2 large eggs
- 1 teaspoon vanilla extract

For the frosting:

- 1/2 cup (115g) unsalted butter
- 1/4 cup (20g) unsweetened cocoa powder
- 6 tablespoons milk
- 1 teaspoon vanilla extract
- 4 cups (500g) powdered sugar
- 1 cup (115g) chopped pecans or walnuts (optional)

Instructions:

1. Preheat Oven and Prepare Pan:
   - Preheat your oven to 350°F (175°C). Grease or line a 10x15-inch baking pan with parchment paper.
2. Make the Cake:
   - In a large mixing bowl, whisk together the all-purpose flour, granulated sugar, baking soda, and salt.
   - In a saucepan, combine the water, butter, and cocoa powder. Bring to a boil, then remove from heat.

- Pour the cocoa mixture over the dry ingredients and mix until well combined.
- Stir in the buttermilk, eggs, and vanilla extract until smooth.
3. Bake the Cake:
    - Pour the batter into the prepared baking pan and spread it out evenly.
    - Bake in the preheated oven for 20-25 minutes, or until a toothpick inserted into the center comes out clean.
4. Make the Frosting:
    - In a saucepan, combine the butter, cocoa powder, and milk. Bring to a boil, then remove from heat.
    - Stir in the vanilla extract and powdered sugar until smooth.
    - If using, stir in the chopped pecans or walnuts.
5. Frost the Cake:
    - Immediately pour the warm frosting over the hot cake, spreading it out evenly with a spatula.
6. Cool and Serve:
    - Allow the cake to cool completely before slicing and serving.
    - Enjoy this moist and chocolatey Texas Sheet Cake with friends and family!

This cake is perfect for gatherings and potlucks, and its rich flavor and moist texture are sure to be a hit with everyone.

Strawberry Rhubarb Pie

Ingredients:

For the pie crust:

- 2 1/2 cups all-purpose flour
- 1 tablespoon granulated sugar
- 1 teaspoon salt
- 1 cup (2 sticks) cold unsalted butter, cut into small cubes
- 1/2 cup ice water

For the filling:

- 3 cups sliced rhubarb (about 1/2-inch thick slices)
- 3 cups sliced strawberries
- 3/4 cup granulated sugar
- 1/4 cup cornstarch
- 1 tablespoon freshly squeezed lemon juice
- 1 teaspoon vanilla extract
- 1/2 teaspoon ground cinnamon
- 1/4 teaspoon ground nutmeg
- 1 egg, beaten (for egg wash)
- 1 tablespoon granulated sugar (for sprinkling)

Instructions:

1. Prepare the Pie Crust:
    - In a large mixing bowl, whisk together the all-purpose flour, granulated sugar, and salt.
    - Add the cold cubed butter to the flour mixture. Use a pastry cutter or your fingers to work the butter into the flour until the mixture resembles coarse crumbs.
    - Gradually add the ice water, 1 tablespoon at a time, mixing with a fork, until the dough comes together.
    - Divide the dough into two equal portions, shape each portion into a disk, wrap them in plastic wrap, and refrigerate for at least 1 hour.

2. Preheat Oven:
   - Preheat your oven to 400°F (200°C). Place a baking sheet in the oven to preheat as well.
3. Make the Filling:
   - In a large mixing bowl, combine the sliced rhubarb, sliced strawberries, granulated sugar, cornstarch, lemon juice, vanilla extract, ground cinnamon, and ground nutmeg. Mix until well combined and the fruit is evenly coated.
4. Roll out the Pie Crust:
   - On a lightly floured surface, roll out one disk of chilled pie dough into a circle large enough to fit into a 9-inch pie dish. Transfer the rolled-out dough to the pie dish and gently press it into the bottom and up the sides.
5. Fill the Pie:
   - Pour the prepared fruit filling into the bottom crust, spreading it out evenly.
6. Roll out the Top Crust:
   - Roll out the second disk of chilled pie dough into a circle large enough to cover the pie. You can leave it whole or cut it into strips for a lattice crust.
7. Assemble the Pie:
   - Place the rolled-out top crust over the filled pie. Trim any excess dough and crimp the edges of the crusts together to seal.
   - If using a whole top crust, make several slits in the top to allow steam to escape during baking.
8. Brush with Egg Wash:
   - Brush the top crust with the beaten egg, then sprinkle with the tablespoon of granulated sugar for a golden finish.
9. Bake:
   - Place the assembled pie on the preheated baking sheet in the oven.
   - Bake for 20 minutes, then reduce the oven temperature to 350°F (175°C) and continue baking for an additional 35-40 minutes, or until the crust is golden brown and the filling is bubbly.
10. Cool and Serve:
    - Allow the pie to cool completely on a wire rack before slicing and serving.
    - Serve slices of Strawberry Rhubarb Pie on their own or topped with a scoop of vanilla ice cream or a dollop of whipped cream for a delicious treat!

Enjoy the sweet-tart combination of strawberries and rhubarb in this classic pie!

Buttermilk Pie

Ingredients:

- 1 9-inch unbaked pie crust
- 1 1/2 cups granulated sugar
- 3 tablespoons all-purpose flour
- 1/4 teaspoon salt
- 1/2 cup (1 stick) unsalted butter, melted
- 3 large eggs
- 1 cup buttermilk
- 1 tablespoon vanilla extract
- 1 tablespoon lemon juice
- Zest of 1 lemon (optional)
- Whipped cream, for serving (optional)

Instructions:

1. Preheat Oven:
    - Preheat your oven to 350°F (175°C). Place the unbaked pie crust in a 9-inch pie dish and set aside.
2. Make the Filling:
    - In a large mixing bowl, whisk together the granulated sugar, all-purpose flour, and salt until well combined.
    - Add the melted unsalted butter to the dry ingredients and mix until smooth.
    - Beat in the eggs one at a time until fully incorporated.
    - Stir in the buttermilk, vanilla extract, lemon juice, and lemon zest (if using) until the filling mixture is smooth and well combined.
3. Pour Filling into Pie Crust:
    - Pour the prepared buttermilk filling into the unbaked pie crust, spreading it out evenly with a spatula.
4. Bake:
    - Place the pie in the preheated oven and bake for 45-50 minutes, or until the filling is set and the top is lightly golden brown.
    - If the crust begins to brown too quickly, you can cover the edges with foil or a pie crust shield halfway through baking.
5. Cool and Serve:

- Remove the pie from the oven and allow it to cool completely on a wire rack.
- Once cooled, slice and serve the Buttermilk Pie at room temperature.
- Optionally, serve slices of the pie with a dollop of whipped cream on top for added richness and flavor.

Enjoy the creamy, tangy sweetness of Buttermilk Pie as a delightful dessert for any occasion!

Coconut Macaroons

Ingredients:

- 3 cups sweetened shredded coconut
- 2/3 cup granulated sugar
- 1/4 teaspoon salt
- 4 large egg whites
- 1 teaspoon vanilla extract

Instructions:

1. Preheat Oven:
    - Preheat your oven to 325°F (160°C). Line a baking sheet with parchment paper or a silicone baking mat.
2. Mix Ingredients:
    - In a large mixing bowl, combine the sweetened shredded coconut, granulated sugar, and salt. Mix well.
3. Whisk Egg Whites:
    - In a separate bowl, whisk the egg whites until they become frothy, but not stiff.
4. Combine with Coconut Mixture:
    - Add the frothy egg whites and vanilla extract to the coconut mixture. Stir until well combined and the coconut is evenly coated with the egg mixture.
5. Shape Macaroons:
    - Using a spoon or cookie scoop, scoop out about 2 tablespoons of the coconut mixture and shape it into a compact mound with your hands.
    - Place the shaped macaroons onto the prepared baking sheet, leaving some space between each one.
6. Bake:
    - Bake in the preheated oven for 20-25 minutes, or until the macaroons are lightly golden brown on the outside.
    - Keep an eye on them towards the end of the baking time to prevent them from over-browning.
7. Cool:
    - Once baked, remove the macaroons from the oven and let them cool on the baking sheet for a few minutes.
    - Transfer the macaroons to a wire rack to cool completely.

8. Optional Chocolate Drizzle:
    - If desired, melt some chocolate (such as semi-sweet or dark chocolate) in a microwave-safe bowl in 30-second intervals, stirring in between, until smooth.
    - Drizzle the melted chocolate over the cooled macaroons, then allow the chocolate to set before serving.
9. Serve and Enjoy:
    - Once the chocolate (if using) has set, serve the coconut macaroons and enjoy their sweet and chewy goodness!
    - Store any leftover macaroons in an airtight container at room temperature for up to several days.

These Coconut Macaroons are perfect for satisfying your sweet tooth and make a delightful treat for any occasion!

Gooey Butter Cake

Ingredients:

For the cake base:

- 1 package (18.25 ounces) yellow cake mix
- 1/2 cup (1 stick) unsalted butter, melted
- 1 large egg

For the gooey butter layer:

- 1 package (8 ounces) cream cheese, softened
- 2 large eggs
- 1 teaspoon vanilla extract
- 1/2 cup (1 stick) unsalted butter, melted
- 4 cups (1 pound) powdered sugar, sifted, plus extra for dusting

Instructions:

1. Preheat Oven:
    - Preheat your oven to 350°F (175°C). Grease a 9x13-inch baking pan or line it with parchment paper.
2. Prepare the Cake Base:
    - In a large mixing bowl, combine the yellow cake mix, melted butter, and egg until well combined.
    - Press the mixture evenly into the bottom of the prepared baking pan to form the cake base.
3. Make the Gooey Butter Layer:
    - In another mixing bowl, beat the softened cream cheese until smooth and creamy.
    - Add the eggs, one at a time, beating well after each addition.
    - Mix in the vanilla extract and melted butter until smooth.
    - Gradually add the powdered sugar, mixing until well combined and smooth.
4. Assemble and Bake:

- Pour the gooey butter mixture over the cake base in the baking pan, spreading it out evenly with a spatula.
- Bake in the preheated oven for 40-45 minutes, or until the edges are golden brown and the center is set but still slightly gooey.

5. Cool and Serve:
    - Remove the cake from the oven and let it cool completely in the pan on a wire rack.
    - Once cooled, dust the top of the cake with powdered sugar.
    - Cut into squares and serve the Gooey Butter Cake at room temperature.
    - Enjoy the rich, creamy texture and sweet flavor of this irresistible dessert!

This Gooey Butter Cake is a classic indulgence that's sure to please your taste buds and satisfy your sweet cravings.

M&M Cookies

Ingredients:

- 1 cup (2 sticks) unsalted butter, softened
- 1 cup granulated sugar
- 1 cup packed light brown sugar
- 2 large eggs
- 1 teaspoon vanilla extract
- 3 cups all-purpose flour
- 1 teaspoon baking soda
- 1/2 teaspoon baking powder
- 1/2 teaspoon salt
- 1 1/2 cups M&M's candies

Instructions:

1. Preheat Oven:
    - Preheat your oven to 350°F (175°C). Line baking sheets with parchment paper or silicone baking mats.
2. Cream Butter and Sugars:
    - In a large mixing bowl, cream together the softened butter, granulated sugar, and brown sugar until light and fluffy.
3. Add Eggs and Vanilla:
    - Beat in the eggs, one at a time, until well combined. Stir in the vanilla extract.
4. Combine Dry Ingredients:
    - In a separate bowl, whisk together the all-purpose flour, baking soda, baking powder, and salt.
5. Mix Wet and Dry Ingredients:
    - Gradually add the dry ingredients to the wet ingredients, mixing until just combined. Be careful not to overmix.
6. Fold in M&M's:
    - Gently fold in the M&M's candies until evenly distributed throughout the cookie dough.
7. Form Dough Balls:

- Using a cookie scoop or spoon, scoop out portions of dough and roll them into balls. Place the dough balls onto the prepared baking sheets, leaving some space between each one for spreading.
8. Bake:
    - Bake in the preheated oven for 10-12 minutes, or until the cookies are lightly golden brown around the edges.
9. Cool:
    - Remove the cookies from the oven and let them cool on the baking sheets for a few minutes before transferring them to wire racks to cool completely.
10. Serve and Enjoy:
    - Once cooled, serve the M&M Cookies and enjoy their colorful appearance and delicious taste!
    - Store any leftover cookies in an airtight container at room temperature for up to several days.

These M&M Cookies are perfect for parties, bake sales, or simply enjoying as a sweet treat any time of day!

Peanut Butter Pie

Ingredients:

For the crust:

- 1 1/2 cups graham cracker crumbs
- 1/4 cup granulated sugar
- 1/2 cup (1 stick) unsalted butter, melted

For the filling:

- 1 cup creamy peanut butter
- 8 ounces cream cheese, softened
- 1 cup powdered sugar
- 1 teaspoon vanilla extract
- 1 cup heavy cream, whipped

For the topping:

- 1/2 cup heavy cream
- 1/4 cup powdered sugar
- 1/4 cup chopped peanuts (optional)

Instructions:

1. Prepare the Crust:
    - In a mixing bowl, combine the graham cracker crumbs, granulated sugar, and melted butter until well mixed.
    - Press the mixture into the bottom and up the sides of a 9-inch pie dish to form the crust. You can use the back of a spoon or your fingers to press it firmly.
2. Chill the Crust:
    - Place the crust in the refrigerator to chill while you prepare the filling.
3. Make the Filling:

- In a large mixing bowl, beat together the creamy peanut butter, softened cream cheese, powdered sugar, and vanilla extract until smooth and well combined.
- In a separate bowl, whip the heavy cream until stiff peaks form.
- Gently fold the whipped cream into the peanut butter mixture until evenly combined and no streaks remain.

4. Fill the Crust:
    - Pour the peanut butter filling into the chilled graham cracker crust, spreading it out evenly with a spatula.
5. Chill the Pie:
    - Place the pie in the refrigerator to chill for at least 4 hours, or until set.
6. Make the Topping:
    - In a mixing bowl, whip the heavy cream and powdered sugar until stiff peaks form.
    - Spread or pipe the whipped cream over the chilled peanut butter pie.
7. Optional Garnish:
    - Sprinkle the chopped peanuts over the whipped cream topping for extra crunch and flavor, if desired.
8. Serve and Enjoy:
    - Slice and serve the Peanut Butter Pie chilled, and enjoy its creamy, indulgent flavor!

This Peanut Butter Pie is sure to be a hit with peanut butter lovers and dessert enthusiasts alike!

Chocolate Eclairs

Ingredients:

For the choux pastry:

- 1/2 cup (1 stick) unsalted butter
- 1 cup water
- 1 cup all-purpose flour
- 1/4 teaspoon salt
- 4 large eggs

For the pastry cream filling:

- 2 cups whole milk
- 1/2 cup granulated sugar
- 4 large egg yolks
- 1/4 cup cornstarch
- 2 tablespoons unsalted butter
- 1 teaspoon vanilla extract

For the chocolate glaze:

- 1/2 cup heavy cream
- 1 cup semisweet chocolate chips

Instructions:

1. Preheat Oven:
    - Preheat your oven to 400°F (200°C). Line a baking sheet with parchment paper or a silicone baking mat.
2. Make the Choux Pastry:
    - In a medium saucepan, combine the unsalted butter and water. Heat over medium heat until the butter is melted and the mixture comes to a boil.
    - Remove the saucepan from the heat and quickly stir in the all-purpose flour and salt until a smooth dough forms.

- Return the saucepan to low heat and continue to cook the dough, stirring constantly, for about 1 minute to slightly dry it out.
- Transfer the dough to a mixing bowl and let it cool for a few minutes.
- Beat in the eggs, one at a time, mixing well after each addition, until the dough is smooth and glossy.

3. Pipe the Eclairs:
    - Transfer the choux pastry dough to a piping bag fitted with a large round tip (or simply cut a corner off a zip-top bag).
    - Pipe 4- to 5-inch lengths of dough onto the prepared baking sheet, leaving some space between each one.
4. Bake:
    - Bake the eclairs in the preheated oven for 15 minutes, then reduce the oven temperature to 350°F (175°C) and continue baking for an additional 20-25 minutes, or until the eclairs are golden brown and puffed up.
    - Remove the eclairs from the oven and let them cool completely on a wire rack.
5. Make the Pastry Cream Filling:
    - In a saucepan, heat the whole milk over medium heat until it just begins to simmer.
    - In a mixing bowl, whisk together the granulated sugar, egg yolks, and cornstarch until smooth.
    - Slowly pour the hot milk into the egg mixture, whisking constantly, to temper the eggs.
    - Return the mixture to the saucepan and cook over medium heat, stirring constantly, until thickened.
    - Remove the saucepan from the heat and stir in the unsalted butter and vanilla extract until smooth.
    - Transfer the pastry cream to a bowl and cover it with plastic wrap, pressing the plastic wrap directly onto the surface to prevent a skin from forming. Let it cool completely.
6. Fill the Eclairs:
    - Once the eclairs and pastry cream are completely cooled, use a piping bag fitted with a small round tip (or simply cut a small hole in the side) to fill each eclair with the pastry cream.
7. Make the Chocolate Glaze:
    - In a small saucepan, heat the heavy cream until it just begins to simmer.
    - Remove the saucepan from the heat and add the semisweet chocolate chips. Let them sit for a minute, then whisk until smooth and glossy.
8. Glaze the Eclairs:

- Dip the top of each eclair into the chocolate glaze, allowing any excess to drip off.
9. Chill and Serve:
    - Place the glazed eclairs on a wire rack to set the chocolate glaze.
    - Once set, serve the Chocolate Eclairs and enjoy their deliciousness!

These Chocolate Eclairs are a delightful treat, perfect for any special occasion or simply as a sweet indulgence!

Blackberry Cobbler

Ingredients:

For the filling:

- 6 cups fresh blackberries
- 3/4 cup granulated sugar
- 1 tablespoon lemon juice
- 1 tablespoon cornstarch

For the topping:

- 1 1/2 cups all-purpose flour
- 1/2 cup granulated sugar
- 1 1/2 teaspoons baking powder
- 1/2 teaspoon salt
- 1/2 cup (1 stick) unsalted butter, chilled and cut into small pieces
- 1/2 cup milk
- 1 teaspoon vanilla extract

Instructions:

1. Preheat Oven:
    - Preheat your oven to 375°F (190°C). Grease a 9x13-inch baking dish or a similar-sized casserole dish.
2. Prepare the Filling:
    - In a large mixing bowl, gently toss together the fresh blackberries, granulated sugar, lemon juice, and cornstarch until the blackberries are coated evenly. Transfer the blackberry mixture to the prepared baking dish and spread it out evenly.
3. Make the Topping:
    - In a separate mixing bowl, whisk together the all-purpose flour, granulated sugar, baking powder, and salt until well combined.
    - Add the chilled pieces of unsalted butter to the flour mixture. Use a pastry cutter or your fingers to work the butter into the dry ingredients until the mixture resembles coarse crumbs.

- In a small bowl, mix together the milk and vanilla extract. Gradually add the milk mixture to the flour mixture, stirring until a thick, sticky dough forms.
4. Top the Cobbler:
    - Drop spoonfuls of the dough mixture evenly over the blackberry filling in the baking dish.
5. Bake:
    - Place the baking dish in the preheated oven and bake for 35-40 minutes, or until the topping is golden brown and the blackberry filling is bubbly.
6. Cool and Serve:
    - Remove the cobbler from the oven and let it cool slightly before serving.
    - Serve the Blackberry Cobbler warm, optionally with a scoop of vanilla ice cream or a dollop of whipped cream on top.

Enjoy the warm, juicy blackberry filling and tender, buttery topping of this delightful Blackberry Cobbler!

Apple Dumplings

Ingredients:

For the pastry:

- 2 cups all-purpose flour
- 1/2 teaspoon salt
- 2/3 cup unsalted butter, chilled and cubed
- 6-8 tablespoons ice water

For the filling:

- 6 medium-sized apples (such as Granny Smith), peeled, cored, and halved
- 1/2 cup granulated sugar
- 1 teaspoon ground cinnamon
- 1/4 teaspoon ground nutmeg
- 1/4 cup unsalted butter, cut into small cubes

For the syrup:

- 1 cup granulated sugar
- 1 cup water
- 1/4 cup unsalted butter
- 1 teaspoon vanilla extract
- 1/2 teaspoon ground cinnamon

Instructions:

1. Preheat Oven:
    - Preheat your oven to 375°F (190°C). Grease a 9x13-inch baking dish or similar-sized baking pan.
2. Make the Pastry:
    - In a large mixing bowl, whisk together the all-purpose flour and salt.
    - Cut in the chilled cubed butter using a pastry cutter or your fingers until the mixture resembles coarse crumbs.

- Gradually add the ice water, 1 tablespoon at a time, mixing with a fork until the dough comes together. You may not need to use all of the water.
- Form the dough into a ball, wrap it in plastic wrap, and refrigerate it while you prepare the filling and syrup.

3. Prepare the Apples:
   - In a small bowl, mix together the granulated sugar, ground cinnamon, and ground nutmeg.
   - Roll out the chilled pastry dough on a floured surface to about 1/8-inch thickness. Cut the dough into squares large enough to wrap around each apple half.
   - Place an apple half on each pastry square. Fill the cavity of each apple half with some of the sugar and spice mixture, then top with a few cubes of butter.
4. Wrap the Apples:
   - Fold the pastry dough up and around each apple half, pinching the seams to seal and forming a dumpling shape.
5. Arrange in Baking Dish:
   - Place the wrapped apple dumplings in the prepared baking dish, seam side down.
6. Make the Syrup:
   - In a saucepan, combine the granulated sugar, water, unsalted butter, vanilla extract, and ground cinnamon. Bring the mixture to a simmer over medium heat, stirring occasionally, until the sugar is dissolved and the butter is melted.
7. Pour Syrup Over Dumplings:
   - Pour the hot syrup mixture over the apple dumplings in the baking dish.
8. Bake:
   - Bake the apple dumplings in the preheated oven for 40-45 minutes, or until the pastry is golden brown and the apples are tender when pierced with a fork.
9. Serve:
   - Serve the apple dumplings warm, optionally with a scoop of vanilla ice cream or a drizzle of caramel sauce on top.

Enjoy the comforting flavors of warm apples and flaky pastry in these delicious Apple Dumplings!

Chocolate Covered Strawberries

Ingredients:

- Fresh strawberries (about 1 pound)
- 8 ounces semi-sweet or dark chocolate, chopped
- Optional: white chocolate, chopped nuts, shredded coconut, sprinkles, or edible gold flakes for decoration

Instructions:

1. Wash the strawberries and pat them dry with paper towels. Make sure they are completely dry before dipping them in chocolate to prevent the chocolate from seizing.
2. Line a baking sheet or tray with parchment paper or wax paper. This will prevent the chocolate-covered strawberries from sticking.
3. Place the chopped chocolate in a heatproof bowl. If using both semi-sweet and white chocolate, place each type in separate bowls.
4. Fill a saucepan with a couple of inches of water and bring it to a simmer over medium heat. Place the bowl of chocolate over the saucepan, making sure the bottom of the bowl doesn't touch the water. This setup creates a makeshift double boiler.
5. Stir the chocolate occasionally with a heatproof spatula until it's completely melted and smooth. Remove the bowl from the heat.
6. Hold a strawberry by the stem or green leaves and dip it into the melted chocolate, swirling it around to coat evenly. Allow any excess chocolate to drip off back into the bowl.
7. Place the chocolate-covered strawberry onto the prepared baking sheet. Repeat the dipping process with the remaining strawberries.
8. If desired, melt the white chocolate using the same method as before. Drizzle the melted white chocolate over the dipped strawberries for a decorative touch.
9. While the chocolate is still wet, you can sprinkle chopped nuts, shredded coconut, sprinkles, or edible gold flakes over the strawberries for added flavor and decoration.
10. Once all the strawberries are dipped and decorated, place the baking sheet in the refrigerator for about 15-30 minutes to allow the chocolate to set.
11. Once the chocolate is set, transfer the chocolate-covered strawberries to a serving platter or plate.

12. Serve the chocolate covered strawberries immediately, or store them in the refrigerator until ready to enjoy. They are best eaten within a day or two.
13. Enjoy your delicious and decadent chocolate covered strawberries!

These chocolate covered strawberries make a beautiful and tasty treat for Valentine's Day, anniversaries, bridal showers, or any other special occasion. They're also a fun activity to make with kids or loved ones.

Rice Krispie Treats

Ingredients:

- 6 cups Rice Krispies cereal
- 1/4 cup (4 tablespoons) unsalted butter
- 1 package (10 ounces) marshmallows (about 40 large marshmallows)

Instructions:

1. Grease a 9x13-inch baking dish with butter or non-stick cooking spray. Set aside.
2. In a large pot, melt the butter over low heat.
3. Once the butter is melted, add the marshmallows to the pot. Stir continuously until the marshmallows are completely melted and smooth. This should take about 3-4 minutes.
4. Remove the pot from the heat and quickly stir in the Rice Krispies cereal until well coated with the marshmallow mixture.
5. Transfer the mixture to the prepared baking dish. Use a spatula or greased hands to press the mixture evenly into the dish.
6. Allow the Rice Krispie Treats to cool and set at room temperature for at least 30 minutes before cutting into squares.
7. Once cooled and set, use a sharp knife to cut the treats into squares or rectangles.
8. Serve and enjoy your homemade Rice Krispie Treats!

Variations:

- Add 1 teaspoon of vanilla extract to the melted marshmallow mixture for extra flavor.
- Stir in 1/2 cup of mini chocolate chips, M&M's, or chopped nuts for added texture and flavor.
- Drizzle melted chocolate or peanut butter over the cooled treats for a decorative touch.
- Use flavored marshmallows, such as strawberry or caramel, for a unique twist on the classic recipe.
- Substitute Rice Krispies cereal with other crispy rice cereals or even crushed graham crackers for different variations.

These homemade Rice Krispie Treats are perfect for parties, potlucks, bake sales, or simply as a delicious snack for any occasion. They're quick to make and always a hit with both kids and adults alike!

Molten Lava Cake

Ingredients:

- 4 ounces (113 grams) semi-sweet chocolate, chopped
- 1/2 cup (115 grams) unsalted butter
- 2 large eggs
- 2 large egg yolks
- 1/4 cup (50 grams) granulated sugar
- 1 teaspoon vanilla extract
- 1/8 teaspoon salt
- 1/4 cup (30 grams) all-purpose flour
- Optional: powdered sugar, vanilla ice cream, or whipped cream for serving

Instructions:

1. Preheat your oven to 425°F (220°C). Grease and flour four ramekins or custard cups. Place them on a baking sheet for easy handling.
2. In a heatproof bowl set over a pot of simmering water (double boiler), melt the chopped chocolate and butter together, stirring occasionally until smooth. Alternatively, you can melt them together in the microwave, stirring every 30 seconds until smooth.
3. In a separate bowl, whisk together the eggs, egg yolks, granulated sugar, vanilla extract, and salt until well combined.
4. Gradually pour the melted chocolate mixture into the egg mixture, whisking constantly until smooth and well combined.
5. Sift the flour over the chocolate mixture and gently fold it in until just combined. Be careful not to overmix.
6. Divide the batter evenly among the prepared ramekins, filling each about 3/4 full.
7. Bake the lava cakes in the preheated oven for 12-14 minutes, or until the edges are set but the centers are still soft and jiggly.
8. Remove the lava cakes from the oven and let them cool in the ramekins for 1-2 minutes.
9. Carefully run a knife around the edges of each lava cake to loosen them from the ramekins. Invert each cake onto a serving plate.
10. Dust the tops of the lava cakes with powdered sugar, if desired. Serve immediately with vanilla ice cream or whipped cream for an extra indulgent treat.
11. Enjoy your homemade molten lava cakes while they're still warm and gooey!

These molten lava cakes are perfect for special occasions, date nights, or anytime you're craving a rich and indulgent chocolate dessert. The best part is breaking into the center to reveal the warm, gooey chocolate lava inside!

Lemon Pound Cake

- 26g) unsalted butter, softened
- 2 cups (400g) granulated sugar
- 4 large eggs, room temperature
- 3 cups (360g) all-purpose flour
- 1/2 teaspoon baking powder
- 1/2 teaspoon baking soda
- 1/2 teaspoon salt
- 1 cup (240ml) buttermilk, room temperature
- Zest of 2 lemons
- 1/4 cup (60ml) fresh lemon juice
- 1 teaspoon vanilla extract

For the lemon glaze:

- 1 cup (120g) powdered sugar
- 2-3 tablespoons fresh lemon juice

Instructions:

1. Preheat your oven to 325°F (160°C). Grease and flour a 10-inch (25cm) bundt pan or tube pan.
2. In a large mixing bowl, cream together the softened butter and granulated sugar until light and fluffy, about 3-4 minutes.
3. Add the eggs, one at a time, beating well after each addition.
4. In a separate bowl, sift together the flour, baking powder, baking soda, and salt.
5. In another bowl, combine the buttermilk, lemon zest, lemon juice, and vanilla extract.
6. Gradually add the dry ingredients to the creamed butter mixture alternately with the buttermilk mixture, beginning and ending with the dry ingredients. Mix until just combined, being careful not to overmix.
7. Pour the batter into the prepared bundt pan, spreading it evenly with a spatula.
8. Bake in the preheated oven for 55-65 minutes, or until a toothpick inserted into the center of the cake comes out clean.
9. Remove the cake from the oven and let it cool in the pan for 10-15 minutes before transferring it to a wire rack to cool completely.

10. While the cake is cooling, prepare the lemon glaze by whisking together the powdered sugar and fresh lemon juice until smooth. Adjust the consistency by adding more lemon juice if needed.
11. Once the cake has cooled completely, drizzle the lemon glaze over the top of the cake.
12. Allow the glaze to set for a few minutes before slicing and serving.
13. Enjoy your delicious and tangy lemon pound cake!

This lemon pound cake is perfect for any occasion, from afternoon tea to dessert at a dinner party. Its bright lemon flavor and dense texture make it a favorite among citrus lovers.

www.ingramcontent.com/pod-product-compliance
Lightning Source LLC
LaVergne TN
LVHW081556060526
838201LV00054B/1924